HAUNTED
WEATHERFORD

TEAL GRAY

Haunted
America

Published by Haunted America
A Division of The History Press
Charleston, SC
www.historypress.com

All images by the author or from the author's collection unless otherwise noted.

First published 2024

Manufactured in the United States

ISBN 9781467154055

Library of Congress Control Number: 2024938193

Notice: The information in this book is true and complete to the best of our knowledge. It is offered without guarantee on the part of the author or The History Press. The author and The History Press disclaim all liability in connection with the use of this book.

CONTENTS

Acknowledgements   5
Introduction   7

1. Parker County Courthouse   15
2. Angel's Nest Bed and Breakfast   18
3. The Davis-Martin Home   32
4. B and H Feed Store   33
5. Weatherford Public Library   36
6. The Baker Mansion   42
7. Twisted Snifter   46
8. Apparitions at Chandor Gardens   50
9. Railroad Ghost Stories   53
10. 1908 Santa Fe Depot   56
11. Weatherford Sanitarium   60
12. Old City Greenwood Cemetery   67
13. Clark Cemetery   75
14. Baker Cemetery   77
15. Spring Creek Cemetery   79
16. Hoggard-Reynolds Cemetery   81
17. Oakland Cemetery   83
18. The Phantom Stagecoach   86
19. 1869 Mason-Built Weatherford College   88
20. Campbell Hospital   91

21. Citizens National Bank   94
22. Weatherford Vintage Car Museum, Event Center,
       and Grill   96
23. Knights of Pythias Lodge   99
24. Franco-Texan Land Company Building   101
25. 202 West Oak Street   104
26. First Monday "Stray Days"   106
27. The Double Cabin at Holland Lake   109
28. Haunted Amusement Park   112
29. Veal's Station and Cemetery   116
30. Haunted Hill House   120

Afterword   125
Bibliography   127
About the Author   128

ACKNOWLEDGEMENTS

Thank you to my family. You are treasures in my heart.

Thank you to everyone who shared their stories and those of their families with me. Your generosity made this book possible.

A special thank-you to folklorist Susan Hill and local historian Donna McCauley, the two best Weatherford natives I know.

Thank you to my dear friend Mark Elliott Fults for your encouragement.

Thanks to my editor, Ben Gibson, who works with Arcadia Publishing and The History Press.

INTRODUCTION

In your lifetime, there will be encounters you can't explain.
That doesn't make them any less real.
—Teal Gray

Writing this book about haunted Weatherford has been an inspiring experience. I have always loved old Westerns and read countless books on how the West was settled by brave, pioneering families who risked their lives. This book brought that to life, with names and stories I now feel connected to and cherish.

Two things that the settlers, pioneers, early merchants, community leaders, and law enforcement had in common were determination and strong faith in God and their fellow community members. These men and women were connectors and uniters, ushering in a new age of ideas and the spirit of innovation. You can teach a trade, but you can't teach inspired works. These men and women were inspired to bond and build businesses and strong communities that would endure. They succeeded in their dreams. I experienced the fulfillment of those inspired dreams of the first residents of Weatherford, Texas, in every building and home still standing that I was blessed to enter and interact with.

These buildings feel like old friends now. I felt the history and lives lived that still breathe within their walls. I love to take a moment standing on the old wooden floors to imagine myself here 150 years ago or more. The creaking floor joints echo through decades of busy shoppers and long-ago times. Moments of great joy are balanced with loss and great sorrow. I am old-fashioned, so many of the items they would shop for are on my list as well—feed sacks, notions, buttons made of pearl, and fabrics in colors not seen in the small towns of the West before being brought over on ships or trains. But while these long-ago residents shopped at the general store for theirs, I have to search in the many antique shops for mine.

A Texas State Historical Marker for Weatherford is at the intersection of Palo Pinto Street U.S. 180 and South Main Street Farm to Market Road 51, on the left, when traveling east on Palo Pinto Street. It reads:

> *Founded 1856. Named for Jefferson Weatherford, state senator and a confederate soldier. Frontier people found protection here from constant Indian threat during Civil War. Long the only town between Fort Worth and El Paso. Home of Chandor Gardens and Texas Railroad Museum. Nearby is the Double Log Cabin Museum.*

I have always loved reading historical markers of all kinds. As a child, whenever we left my birthplace in Dallas, Texas, to visit family in San Angelo, Texas, I pestered my father to stop at every marker on the way. This never happened, but I have read quite a few. Reading the marker for Weatherford made me realize that as a child, my imagination ate up the sometimes harrowing stories like candy; now, I read them with more compassion and a sense of awe at the adventures and struggles they depict. This marker has a sentence that really made me think: "Long the only town between Fort Worth and El Paso." That is 575 miles. If you owned a horse and could ride at a good pace of 25 miles daily, you would make it in twenty-three days. That is, if your horse stayed well, you stayed well, the weather wasn't bad, a snake didn't bite you or your horse, and you weren't killed by people who could do so for any number of reasons. It would take longer if you were in a wagon, even if the wheel didn't break. On foot, it was even longer if you were in good health and uninjured. It would be eight and a half hours by car if you didn't stop. Add in the many real-life perilous situations those early travelers faced, and it took grit.

Pioneer ghost stories didn't always happen in a house, building, or barn. Many experiences occurred outdoors. More than one family I spoke with had a version of a ghostly encounter centered on the chuckwagons on cattle drives and the bigger ranches. Workdays were not eight hours but more like eighteen to twenty, so sleep was valuable and rarely wasted on pranks. Back then, you would more likely than not get shot by surprising someone.

Parker County Post #163 ruins.

Chuckwagon cooks, or "cookies" as they were playfully called, had even stranger hours, as they had to have the first meal ready for the ranch hands and cowboys generally at 4:00 a.m. The menu would depend on location and available funds before they set out on the trail. Biscuits were a staple.

Some of the best cooks would make gravy worth fighting for. If the bacon ran out, you might get some lard to dip it in and some strong coffee. As the men ate quickly, the cook and his helper would pack up and move ahead of the cattle to an estimated spot where they'd stop for supper (most call it lunch these days). The cowboys would eat and nap while the cook and helper moved ahead again and prepared dinner. This routine is common to all ranches and cattle drives.

The second night of the cattle drive, around two o'clock in the morning, the cook and helper were stealing the last moments of sleep before the work began when the blankets were pulled off both men. Startled awake and not understanding what happened, they got out of the opposite ends of the wagon to find the culprit. There must be one, right? No one was close. Cook asked the helper if any of the guys saw anyone. They had not. Hard work makes for a good distraction.

Over the next two nights, sightings of a man in an odd green coat and another in a beaver skin hat were spotted right before or after the cattle spooked, and the all-important campfire unexplainably went out after being at a full blaze. The men's belongings were disheveled every time they returned from their work. They were tired and fighting among themselves as their nerves frayed more each day.

The company had never driven this trail before because of fear of outlaw ambushes and attacks from Native Americans. So, everyone's hearts were in their throats when a cowboy rode into camp for his life, it seemed. He claimed he saw two men crouched by the river. He called to them, and when they turned, they were more skeletons than men. Their faces were bloody, and one man's hat blew off to reveal that he had been scalped. That's an unmistakable wound. The men in the camp were already riding out at a full run upon hearing this news. The light of day hit the creek, and the men turned as pale as the two skeletons they saw, broken on the rocks and lying half in the water. Animals had feasted on their bodies, and most of their skeletons were gone. There were no horses, but saddles were stacked, and the tie-up rope was still tied between two trees. The bright green coat seen by the campfire the night before was ravaged but unmistakable on the scalped man's body. A beaver skin hat was caught in the brush and torn. Everyone was in disbelief. These were phantoms. The camp had been harassed for days by what they thought were thieves. These men may have been just that, but they also had been dead for months.

The cowboys gathered the rope, saddles, clothing, and anything else they could salvage. When they got to the next town, the cattle were in the sale pens, and their job for the moment was complete. They turned the recovered materials over to the sheriff in hopes that the men might have family searching for them and that the unusual hat and coat would be memorable. They would all remember them.

THE CONFLICT BETWEEN TEXAS colonists and Mexico occurred between October 1835 and April 1836. In 1855, the Texas state legislature established Parker County and named it after pioneer and state representative Isaac Parker, who happened to be Cynthia Ann Parker's uncle.

Cynthia Ann Parker lived through two massacres. She was first kidnapped at Old Fort Parker, just 131 miles from Weatherford, Texas. When she was thirty-three years old, the Battle of Pease River took place near Vernon, Oklahoma, 149 miles from Weatherford. Cynthia was taken prisoner by the whites, who believed her to be a Native American, until they noticed her blue eyes and her blonde hair. Her uncle Isaac Parker took her to his home, but Cynthia could never settle back into the life stolen from her at such a young age. She was forty-three years old when she passed away in 1870. She lived among the Comanches and was the mother of Chief Quanah Parker.

A Texas State Marker erected for Isaac reads:

To the memory of Isaac Parker, Pioneer, soldier, and lawmaker. Born April 7, 1793, in Elbert County, Georgia. Came to Texas in 1833. Served in Elisha Clapp's Company in 1836. Member of Congress of the Republic of Texas, 1839–1845; of the Constitutional Convention in 1845. State Senator. Died April 14, 1883, in Parker County.

I feel more than ever through my research the gratitude for the lawmen who kept the peace in the old Western towns where cattle thieves, gunfighters, bandits, and outlaw gangs often were stared down by one brave sheriff putting his life literally in the gap between the outlaw and the townspeople he was sworn to protect. Now, lawyers would hash out differences, and they did so then. But one thing we can only try to imagine is thundering hooves and one thousand pounds of horseflesh coming at you at forty miles an hour, carrying a rider sometimes shooting at you with two guns, determined to take your life and anything he wanted in your town and knowing you are the only thing keeping the innocent children, women, and men safe. This must have taken unimaginable bravery. It doesn't mean they lacked fear or even shook in their boots. They may have, but they kept the peace anyway, afraid or not.

People who knew I was writing about Weatherford were eager to share this tale of the sheriff who never sleeps. It's been passed down through several families I spoke with. The legend I have heard is that of a shadowy figure thought to be a past sheriff who still keeps the peace long after supposedly resting in it. Some have seen a glint of his sheriff's star badge as he moves silently through the downtown streets. "His hat was pulled down, and his long coat flowed behind him." This is the description most often used when asked what people saw. They say they heard the metallic jingle that spurs make when you walk. The louder the sound, the more determined one walks. I love that he is watching over the town he once protected. Get 'em, Sheriff.

Legendary cattle drivers Oliver Loving, Charles Goodnight, and Bose Ikard rest in the old Greenwood Cemetery in Weatherford. The story of Loving and Goodnight inspired Larry McMurtry's novel *Lonesome Dove*, which has become an iconic piece of Texas literature. The town celebrates its Western heritage with several events throughout the year, including the Goodnight-Loving Festival, which offers Western arts, crafts, and activities. The Parker County Frontier Days and Sheriff's Posse Rodeo is one of the largest rodeos in Texas. I have friends who have visited from all over the state to get a glimpse of a real Texas rodeo and what it must have been like to be a real cowboy at both of these fantastic events.

There is a Texas State Historical Marker for many buildings you will see when visiting. Two places in particular, a bank and a post office, would have been paramount for the growth and livability of the town, as they are to us today. The marker at the Merchants and Farmers State Bank reads:

Chartered on January 22, 1889, as the Merchants and Farmers National Bank of Weatherford, this institution opened for business on March 15, 1889, with capital of $100,000. In 1909 the bank's directors voted to apply for a state charter, and the institution's name was changed to Merchants and Farmers State Bank.

Originally located on the southwest corner of the town square, the bank has occupied this site on the northeast corner since 1893–94. Early leaders of the bank included E.H. Eddleman, President from 1889 to 1915; W.R. Woodhouse, President from 1915 to 1919; and J.H. Doss, Sr., President from 1919 to 1945.

The Merchants and Farmers State Bank has played an important role in Parker County's history as the primary lending source for many agricultural

Old oil building ruins.

enterprises, local businesses, and home mortgages. The bank has maintained a strong civic commitment since its founding and supports a number of community and charitable activities. Continued growth over the years has led to the construction of modern banking facilities. Renamed Texas Bank in 1986, this bank has contributed to the growth and development of Parker County for over a century.

While banks have always been important, so are post offices. Weatherford, for its first decade, was the principal frontier settlement in North Texas between the Trinity and Brazos Valleys. The town was incorporated in 1858, and a post office was opened in 1859. The Weatherford stagecoach stop was midway between Fort Worth and Fort Belknap. This stop was vital to residents and nearby towns as a place to get their mail, packages, and supplies; even medicine for physicians had to be delivered.

The marker for Weatherford's post office at 117 Fort Worth Highway reads:

A postal station was first established in Weatherford in 1856. Facilities were located in several early buildings before this structure was completed in 1914. Judge J.M. Richards was the postmaster at the time. Built on the site of a gasoline service station and an earlier wagon yard, the post office building was designed in the Classical Revival style. Prominent features include arched windows, quoins, a massive portico with columns, and an elaborate cornice topped by a balustrade.

Weatherford acted as the county seat and a safe place for Parker County settlers to rush to until the Indian raids ended in the 1870s. Things finally became peaceful, and you can see examples of society's progress in the homes the settlers built for themselves. There are around sixty examples of different structural styles of homes built in Weatherford, including my all-time favorites, Queen Anne–style homes, and many people's wished-for style, the Victorian. The buildings are a mix of more primitive early structures, more elaborate wooden ones with gingerbread-style accents, and massive brick buildings that seem unshakable against the passing of time.

Now, about all those Weatherford ghosts…

Chapter 1
Parker County Courthouse

604 NORTH MAIN STREET
817-598-6168

Another town legend is that of the haunted courthouse. The 1884 building you see now is the fourth structure of Parker County limestone; it is located in its geographical center. It is in the middle of a fast-paced traffic circle with cars and trucks honking and whizzing by. This Second Empire–style courthouse is the heart of downtown and the entire community. The first courthouse was built in 1856 with lumber sourced over three hundred miles away. The second building was a larger two-story building and stood for nearly sixteen years until burning with most of the county records. The third try was built in 1879 but lasted only five years before being lost to yet another fire. On July 10, 1884, during the construction of this current building, a construction worker, Joseph Murray, fell to his death and is said to haunt it to this day.

One of the most talked-about ghostly happenings at the Weatherford Courthouse is the mysterious figure often seen wandering the halls, described as a shadowy figure in old-fashioned attire. Witnesses have reported feeling a chill in the air when encountering this spectral presence. Some believe it to be the ghost of a former judge. As this courthouse has one of the largest courtrooms in the state, it served as a place of upholding justice until you were much farther into West Texas lands. Having had so many legal cases and people come through its doors, there could be any number of ghosts that visit or linger in this place. We are all made up of energy, and we leave

Weatherford Courthouse, 1950s. *Postcard made for Corcanges Drug Store.*

Postcard, 1960s. *Stryker's Western Fotocolor.*

residual amounts of it in places where we experience great joy and great sorrow. All these emotions, along with dread and fear, could be trapped in its walls and felt by visitors in its historic halls. The feeling so overcame one woman I spoke with that she was convinced something ominous began walking up the stairs behind her, moving closer to her side, and following her when she was in the building in the late 1990s. She went to a Catholic church to be blessed so the entity would not follow her home, and she was not even of that faith. Knowing this woman to be very stable and with a no-nonsense personality makes me believe her story without question. It still scares her to speak about it.

This structure underwent a major renovation in 2003, and the changes were met with more rumored hauntings and paranormal activity. Ghosts don't like change, and activity is often reported as more frequent and sometimes more aggressive following renovations of any size. I believe spirits are trying to protect their space, not meaning any actual harm.

Visitors have also reported hearing disembodied voices and footsteps echoing through the empty corridors, even when the building is closed to the public. Doors have been known to slam shut on their own, and lights flicker inexplicably, adding to the courthouse's eerie atmosphere.

Keep your eyes peeled and your senses sharp; you never know when you might encounter one of the ghostly inhabitants who call this historic building home.

The Texas Historical Marker on the building reads:

> *Scene of many noted trials. Built 1884–86. Cost $55,555.55. Fourth courthouse in history of county, organized 1856. An oak on Ft. Belknap Road was court site that year. In this building practiced S.W.T. Lanham, who was governor of Texas 1902–1906.*

CHAPTER 2
ANGEL'S NEST BED AND BREAKFAST

1105 PALO PINTO
817-596-8295

My ghostly lineup for this property numbers at least five. First, the lady in pink, possibly a former owner associated with the living room and upstairs balcony, may be responsible for tapping her nails on the stained-glass door on the room four balcony. Second, a great-smelling dapper man in gray trousers is in room number two. Third on my list is the former resident electrician in room number four. Room number ten is where a male is seen and felt; I think he is the man who was killed in the room by the second owner of the house after discovering the dead body of a prostitute in a peach dress that also haunts room number ten.

This beautiful Queen Anne–style mansion is my absolute favorite place in Weatherford. The original owner, Cornelius Daniel Hartnett, who had an ambitious and successful life, built it with great thought and planning in 1896. Once he settled in Weatherford, he actively helped the town grow. He served on the school board and was one of the originators of the Weatherford Water, Light, and Ice Company.

He was born on September 13, 1851, in County Limerick, Ireland, to Daniel T. Hartnett and Honora Donoghue Hartnett. He was one of eight children. Cornelius and his family immigrated to New York in 1863, when he was twelve. In early adulthood, he contracted with his father, Daniel, for railroads throughout Iowa, Illinois, Missouri, Kansas, Nebraska, Minnesota, and the Dakotas on the Rock Island, Union Pacific, and Chicago, Burlington,

Angel's Nest Bed and Breakfast.

and Quincy Railroad companies, among others. Daniel started as a small businessman contracting on the extensions for the Rock Island Railroad going west from Grinnell, Iowa. Within a short time, he had grown to become one of the largest railroad contractors in the United States. Daniel passed away in Weatherford on July 15, 1891, at age sixty-four.

When Cornelius turned twenty-seven in 1878, he stopped working with his father and worked as a clerk in a grocery store in Whitesboro, Texas, with a monthly starting salary of forty dollars. By the end of his first year there, he was the store manager. In 1880, just two years after the start of this new venture, he became one of the owners. He later partnered with A.F. Starr, and when Starr retired in 1890, the name was changed to C.D. Hartnett and Company, and Cornelius was the sole owner. The company is still in business to this day.

In his personal life, he was a Democrat and belonged to the Catholic faith, as did all his family. He was married twice. His first wife, Kate Byrne, was wed to him in Whitesboro, Texas. They had two sons, Dan and Jefferson, before Kate passed away in 1881. He married a second time in 1883 to Savina Byrne and had four more children: Leo, Jefferson (named in memory of the son who passed from his first marriage), Mary, and Lillian.

Opposite: Belinda Brown in room ten, Angel's Nest.

Left: Looking down the haunted stairway.

His sister Augustine was a nun at Ursuline Convent in Dallas, and his brother Jeffrey became a priest. In 1899, an outbreak of smallpox occurred in Dallas. Jeffrey Aloysius Hartnett, the first priest ordained in and for the Catholic Diocese of Dallas, cared for people who contracted smallpox and were isolated from the public at the pesthouse located six miles from his diocese. A pesthouse was a place where people with a disease were isolated in hopes that others in the population would not catch it. Jeffrey wanted to ensure their spiritual needs were being met. On the night of February 11, 1899, a blizzard hit Dallas like never before. The upper Colorado, Trinity, and Brazos Rivers were frozen solid. Reverend Father Hartnett walked six miles during the worst part of the blizzard to administer last rites to a dying woman. Sadly, he contracted smallpox and died on March 7, 1899. He became a folk hero known as a "martyr to duty" and was the inspiration for many poems and stories.

With Candice Dyer, the current owner, at the helm, this property offers so much to the community beyond just a place to sleep. It hosts weddings, family reunions, retreats, and many romantic celebrations. There is space for special dinners accommodating up to forty people, and the grounds are perfect for strolling on a quiet evening.

Angel's Nest has twenty-nine rooms in total—ten bedrooms, ten bathrooms—and over ten thousand square feet of historic luxury. There are four sets of ten-foot-tall pocket doors and five fireplaces, whose mantels are believed to have been made in Italy. There is a three-story turret soaring from the first to the third floor. You will see a photo in this story of the current owner, Candice Dyer, working high atop ladders at the very tip of the turret—too high for my nerves. Add a wine cellar, hot tubs, wraparound porches, and over one-hundred-year-old oak trees to daydream under, and you will have the much-loved Angel's Nest Bed and Breakfast.

Angel's Nest is unique in its placement in town, just one mile from the historic and haunted downtown courthouse. It is situated on the highest point in Parker County, which gives incredible views from the rooms. Seven even have oversized jacuzzi tubs. Two have fireplaces. Six rooms have balconies with rocking chairs so you can enjoy the beautiful parklike acres. There are many restaurants and attractions nearby to pass your time, but you'll want to linger within this mansion's historic walls. Each room is so beautifully decorated; I've never been to a bed-and-breakfast that was more carefully cared for. No wonder there are so many ghosts. Why would you ever leave a place like this?

Candice Dyer and her right hand, Belinda Brown, are so friendly and welcoming to everyone who enters this home. When I first visited this beautiful mansion, I felt so welcome, from when I spoke with Candice on the phone to when Belinda led my tour and my visit ended. I appreciated that. They are very gracious ladies, and I can see why so many of their guests are return visitors. Belinda helped me sort out all of the ghostly tales. I have heard from many people who couldn't wait to return and stay, which tells you that while they may have been startled by a ghostly sighting, nobody has ever felt truly afraid or in danger. Well, except for the honeymooners in room number ten, that is. All of these spirits are part of this house's history in one way or another and want to stay connected.

While I waited for Belinda to tour the property, my attention was drawn to a mirror in the living room. I went over to it and stared at it for several minutes. I didn't see anything unusual and had not yet heard the stories associated with the living room and that mirror. I can't wait to go back again and see if I can hear the rhythmic click of high heels across the wooden floors and maybe catch a glimpse of the former lady of the house in her pink grandeur. Here are the ghost stories of the previous owner.

Owner Candice Dyer working up high on the Angel's Nest roof. *Photo by the Dyer family.*

A gardener waiting in the living room to be paid had a visual encounter. While looking into the living room mirror, he was startled by a woman he knew was not Candice walking toward him. The gardener said the woman wore a pink long-sleeved, high-necked formal dress. He said she had dishwater blonde hair worn in a bun and was wearing gold-rimmed glasses. He saw her on two occasions while working there.

Opposite: Entryway to Angel's Nest.

Right: Room two, where a man in gray slacks has been seen in the bedroom and bathroom.

In the following years, different guests reported unusual noises and sightings of the same apparition. Candice said it wasn't until hearing a couple describe encountering the vision in pink that the story came together for her. A female guest claimed at morning checkout that she had "visited with the lady of the home she met on the balcony." The guest said the woman had just "stood there and listened" as she went on about how much they were enjoying their stay. The visitor described the woman wearing a pink long-sleeved, high-necked formal dress and having dishwater blonde hair in a bun and gold-rimmed glasses. Candice realized they were describing the same woman.

While working in her basement office, Candice heard someone in high heels walking across the wooden boards on the first floor. The sound of clicking heels continued down the hallway to different rooms and eventually stopped in the living room. While she was awaiting the police, the walking could still be heard. When the officer entered the home via the front door keypad access, he found no windows or doors disturbed and no one else inside.

Could this also be the lady in pink, possibly a prior owner still overseeing her home, even though this encounter was only an auditory phenomenon?

Another time, police were called to the mansion at nightfall. Candice heard a loud crash upstairs. When the police arrived, they found that the crash had come from the laundry room. Everything placed on two shelves was knocked off onto the floor, and no one else was in the house.

Let's move to room number two. This beautiful room has a king-size four-poster bed with an iron canopy, a fifty-inch television above the fireplace, a six-foot antique claw-footed bathtub, beautiful hardwood floors, a breakfast table, a coffee maker, and a small refrigerator to make you feel right at home. It even has a little red heart-shaped pillow on the bed and exudes love from the moment you walk in. It also has a private covered twenty-by-twenty-foot porch with an inviting jacuzzi hot tub that seats six, as well as beautiful wicker furniture and futons to relax on. I can't imagine a better spot for a girls' weekend.

The main sightings in this room seem to belong to a man seen in gray slacks in the bathroom. Once, when the bathroom was being cleaned, Belinda saw a man's legs and gray trousers sitting in a chair, and she could smell a whiff of his cologne. The scent of that cologne is very particular. Belinda remembered smelling that same scent somewhere else and finding out that it was a very expensive cologne. He must have been doing very well for himself during his lifetime. One thing to note is that room number two used to be a dining room. So, it's hard to say if this dapper ghost is that of somebody who stayed in that room or was visiting the dining room from another space. Either way, this is that ghost's favorite area of the house.

Even Belinda's dog can see him. The dog refuses to enter when that spirit is in the room. This is something that I often hear when interviewing people who have had paranormal experiences at different locations, homes, and buildings: their pets, even guard dogs in some locations, refuse to enter certain rooms or parts of a building if spirits are present. All animals, not just dogs, can see spirits or feel when they are around. Animals can also sense the temperament or mood of a person or spirit from the electromagnetic or aura field surrounding them. With the right equipment, you can see the colors in one's aura and connect that to its mood.

In room number three, a woman's and a man's voices have been heard. This room is right by the kitchen. People hear footsteps here and sometimes get frightened. Once, a couple stayed in the room and complained to Belinda that the footsteps kept walking around upstairs. They heard them coming from the room above. On this occasion, Belinda herself was staying

A man was seen by Belinda Brown in this chair.

in that room above them. She had been in bed the whole time, and nobody was walking in there. The creaking noises and hearing footsteps could not be explained. Belinda and the cleaning lady also heard footsteps in this room, but not overhead; it sounded as though somebody was walking across the floorboards beside them. This occurrence happens day or night and frequently.

Room four has a particular ghost connected to the scent of burning wires. There is also a connection to this ghost with room number nine. An apparition of a man in workman's clothes who used to work at the mansion when it was first built is seen kneeling as if working on an electrical plug. He stayed in room number four during his employment at the mansion. The most exciting attribution to this spirit is that he was the electrician in charge

Left: Room three. Guests hear footsteps and have left in the middle of the night.

Below: A former employee is thought to haunt the Angel's Nest. *Photo by the Dyer family.*

of all the electrical work on the property at that time. This gives a fantastic connection story between his life's work and the paranormal experiences attributed to him. It is rare, but I love it when a particular haunting can be connected in this way to a known person who lived or worked in the home.

Room number four has an additional unexplained occurrence. The balcony door is covered with beautiful stained glass. A lady's nails have been heard tapping on that glass. When investigated, nobody was there, but the definite tapping of a woman's nails on the glass is heard in that room from the balcony.

Doppelganger voices are spirits mimicking a live person's voice. This paranormal phenomenon has been heard in room number four. On several occasions, people who know Belinda's distinctive voice very well believed it was Belinda speaking to them from that room. Even the owner, Candice, thought Belinda was speaking to her, but she found the room empty when she entered. Belinda was on an entirely different floor at the time.

One time, when Belinda was giving a tour of that room, only some people within the group said they smelled something burning like wires, and of course, everybody started looking at the plug outlets to be sure everything was in good order. This is common in paranormal investigations, where only certain persons in a group perceive, smell or see paranormal phenomena. While this was just a tour of a beautiful historic mansion, if it had been a paranormal investigation, this would have been written down to mark an occurrence when a particular spirit was creating a scent associated with them in some way to let others know that it was in the room. We like to be noticed and remembered; this trait remains when we die. People's personalities stay with them even when they cross over. I think the electrician was very proud to have worked in this grand home and wants to be remembered as part of its construction.

Room number five has some ghostly cold spots and the feeling of someone else being in the room with you, but it boasts an enormous balcony with a futon that overlooks the breathtaking three and a half acres, so you might not mind. There's a sofa with dual recliners and everything you need to make your stay perfect. People who have spent the night there have noted this room as very relaxing.

Room number ten takes the prize for beauty and hauntings. Five beautiful windows, eight feet tall, surround the bedroom and bathroom. Stained-glass windows surround the huge jacuzzi tub, seven feet by four feet, which holds 142 gallons of water. Can you believe that? With the telescope in your room, you can see twenty-five miles away.

Left: Room ten.

Right: The attic door at Angel's Nest.

Candice tells the story of a honeymooning couple who stayed in room number ten. The man was big in stature, a sailor; you wouldn't assume he would be frightened of anything. He and his bride left in the middle of the night, drove down the street, and called Candice, saying, "I think you might be in danger," suggesting she leave the house. They added that they would not return to the house until daylight for their belongings. The husband assured Candice that he and his bride were sound asleep when a crash sent them sitting straight up in bed. He was unshakable in his belief that someone had entered the room through one of the turret's third-story windows. Candice said that was impossible since the windows were painted and caulked shut and locked down by screws.

The apparition of a lady in a peach dress has become a well-known sighting in room number ten. Belinda had a rare paranormal experience there: she felt the lady in peach walk right through her body. The story attached to this spirit centers on the mansion's second owner and his love of playing on the wild side. He would send his wife and family on shopping trips out of town so he could have the house all to himself. One time, while the family was away, he threw his usual wild party, but things got out of hand. A guest killed a woman in a peach dress who was brought to the party for entertainment purposes. The owner discovered her dead body wearing a peach dress in the turret bathroom above room number ten. The owner then killed the party guest responsible for the murder right there in the same room. Two murders happened in room number ten during that party. Since that fateful night, the lady in the peach dress has haunted the room where she lost her life. The man who murdered her has made his presence known in room number ten as well. The shadow of a man has been seen coming down the stairs from the turret bathroom.

The attic door by room number ten always stays locked. On occasions, it has been heard rattling, as if someone wanted out. Another incident with the attic door happened to the maid while cleaning upstairs. That locked door flew open at her, giving her quite a shock.

White orbs have been seen in the basement. To those who saw them, they looked as if they were dancing. I have experienced this with white orbs in a historic hotel in Missouri. They moved purposefully, gently gliding from place to place. I asked them questions and asked them to move to different locations in the room, and they did. It was a very touching experience. White orbs are associated with good and protective spirits. This makes sense because Angel's Nest has nothing dark or menacing in or around the property. People and organizations ask for my opinion on these matters, so I feel confident in saying it's a blessed (albeit haunted) property.

The property's name is appropriate; many believe white orbs are angelic protectors or guardian spirits. Maybe some of the Hartnett family who visited their brother's home and spent their lives serving God still bless Angel's Nest from heaven.

CHAPTER 3
THE DAVIS-MARTIN HOME

314 WEST OAK STREET

Mary Martin, a famed Broadway star known for portraying Peter Pan, was born on December 1, 1913, in Weatherford. Her parents were Preston Martin, an attorney, and Juanita Presley Martin, a violin teacher at Weatherford College. Her mother became a violin teacher at the age of seventeen. Mary lived in the home built for banker Will Davis in 1918, which her father purchased in 1924 for their family.

Her son Larry Hagman, who also became a well-known actor for his role as J.R. Ewing in the television show *Dallas*, lived in the same house as a child. I had the opportunity to meet Larry while working as a movie extra in *Dallas: The Early Years*, a 1986 American made-for-television drama film and a prequel to the *Dallas* television series. In the film's opening sequence, Larry Hagman appears as his character, J.R. Ewing, being interviewed by a reporter researching the Barnes-Ewing feud in the series.

Mary Martin spoke fondly of her childhood home, a happy place where she felt safe and loved. The house had thirteen-inch-thick cast concrete walls, which provided safety and kept her secrets. It is said that Mary kept a diary hidden in a second-story window box. Wouldn't it be wonderful to know if she dreamed of being the beloved actress she became?

There are rumors that the Peter Pan star still visits her childhood home. Some of the lifelong residents of Weatherford have claimed to see a face in the window upstairs in Mary's bedroom, and odd light anomalies have been seen by late-night passersby. A light or some say possibly an orb trails past the upstairs windows far too quickly to be a living being—unless they can walk through walls, of course. These claims cannot be proven but endure to this day.

CHAPTER 4
B AND H FEED STORE

The B and H Feed Store sits in the historic downtown square of Weatherford. In speaking with the owner, Monte Brantley, he confirmed for me that at one time, this still-in-use building built in 1890 was an old hotel. I've heard stories about this old hotel and was excited to speak to someone else who knew about this building's historic past. It is always lovely to speak with someone who appreciates the history of their town and the homes or businesses they own.

Many different companies have used the old building over the years in addition to its being one of the early hotels in town. Southwestern Bell Telephone Company operated out of the building. Then, a parts company was established, followed by the Merritt Feed Store, owned by Charles F. "Rick" Merritt for over forty years. This era of the building's history is when Monte comes into play. He worked for Merritt through the late 1980s and into the early 1990s, when Monte bought the business he loved, the building and the land it sits on. It still operates as a feed store, and if I were Monte, with as much history as has transpired in that location, I would probably bottle up some of that historic dirt the building sits on and sell it. Can you imagine what that place has seen and experienced from its earliest times, more than 130 years ago?

As it was a hotel in the days of pioneers, outlaws, and founding families, tales have circulated through generations of the many people who stayed or worked there. Maybe their spirits are trying to tell us some of those stories in whispered conversation late at night when it's so quiet, but you can't quite make out what they are saying.

Monte lived upstairs for six years, during which time he experienced some things I was told about the building in its early days as a hotel. These include thinking he saw something and sometimes someone moving past—just a flash out of the corner of his eye here and there. Items were moved, and unexplained noises almost seemed to be trying to get his attention. And there were those darn shadows everyone who has experienced them wish they could unsee moving across the walls. Monte said he never felt afraid of the happenings; he just chalked it up to living and working in a historic space. These things can't be explained and are just part of the building's ongoing life story.

Monte was lucky to have met somebody who worked in the building when it was a bottling company. They told him that back in the day, on the north side of the building, people used to line up and watch workers bottle sodas and other drinks from outside. It would have been thrilling to see such an operation back then. I can imagine men, women and children passing the long summer days daydreaming of tasting a cold bottle of soda from that company.

The owner of the bottling company was R.J. Norton, who lived with his family just a seventeen-minute stroll from his then-bottling company. Monte's daughter Elisa found pieces of old bottles and glass on the property but has yet to find an intact bottle. Elisa kept searching and purchased an intact bottle from when the building was the R.J. Norton Bottling Company and gave it to her father as a present. I think that's pretty amazing.

The Norton home still stands at 406 West Columbia Street. Robert James Norton was one of eight children and is said to be the first white person born in Weatherford, on March 18, 1858. His wife, Ida Potter, descended from some well-known pioneers. One was Robert Potter, a senator in the Texas Congress who was noted for signing the Texas Declaration of Independence and being the first secretary of the Texas navy.

Rather than making their home the priority, Robert completed the construction of the carriage house at the rear of the property first. The Norton mansion took three years to complete and was finally ready in 1907. I am sure he thought this was a logical decision because, from what I understand from interviewing a person who met one of his employees from the bottling company, he was methodical and had well-thought-out plans, so things ran smoothly and efficiently.

Robert's father, Judge David Owen Norton, was one of Weatherford's earliest pioneers and is on the Republic of Texas Poll List of 1846. In 1856, he was appointed U.S. postmaster for Weatherford, Parker, Texas.

Then, in 1859, David became the sole owner of the *Frontier News*, published in Weatherford until the old press and all the materials in the office were destroyed during the Civil War. Robert apprenticed at his father's newspaper in his youth. Later, he became a printer for the *Houston Post*. I was surprised to find twenty-one different newspapers published in the immediate area of Weatherford.

The Weatherford Bottling Company, widely remembered as R.J. Bottling Company, was founded in 1891 and bottled all flavors of soda water, flavoring extracts, syrups, cider, mineral waters, wash bluing, and so on. It also manufactured those delicious soft drinks we spoke about earlier. In 1918, Robert sold his bottling company to Coca-Cola, separating him and the company from the historic old building on North Main Street. Since its construction, the family home at 406 West Columbia Street has remained in the family line.

CHAPTER 5

WEATHERFORD PUBLIC LIBRARY

1014 CHARLES STREET

The Weatherford Public Library has a local history section and genealogy room considered one of the best in Parker County and Texas. I have found fantastic research there that I could not find elsewhere. There also have been several times when I was alone in the genealogy room and felt a presence near me as I was researching. The presence of someone looking over my shoulder was enough for me to turn around more than once. I changed where I was sitting, and it helped, but once more, before I left, it happened again. Maybe it was a past librarian or someone connected with my research offering their help. I'm not the only one who has felt an unseen presence near them in the genealogy room or among the many shelves of books housed within the library. People have reported feeling like they were being watched or followed as they searched for a particular book on their list. Nobody, including myself, ever felt afraid; it was more of a feeling that something or someone was just curious and was ready to help if needed. You may encounter a helpful ghost when you visit.

In front of the genealogy room is a display of dinosaur bones found in the area. I love how the bones are displayed and explain about the species found. The skeleton is that of a tenontosaur or sinew lizard from the early Cretaceous period, the last of three periods in the Mesozoic Era, beginning 145 million years ago and ending 66 million years ago.

If you know me, you know I love dinosaurs. My grandfather Jess discovered one in West Texas. He was working on a ranch when he saw

Weatherford Public Library interior.

Research room at Weatherford Public Library.

Weatherford Public Library.

part of a tusk sticking out of the ground in the wash basin area of the creek. There was a spring three hundred yards up the creek, and it had washed the dirt away from the bones. Beside an eight-foot-long section of tusk, he found a six-inch-long tooth and several other bones. He said he dug down, uncovering part of the carcass and some head bones. He believed it was a prehistoric mastodon. Pools of quicksand stood guard over the site, and he had to pull cattle out of it constantly. My grandfather thought there might have been even more quicksand in that area millions of years ago, and the dinosaur became trapped and eventually the quicksand dried up, preserving the animal's body.

My grandfather told me that the ranch and creek were haunted. He had encounters with what he thought were trespassers camping by the creek, but they were only ghosts evaporating into mist before his eyes. On more than one occasion, he saw a young Native American on horseback looking out into the distance over the lands, always on the same ridgeline. After chasing after the ghost on horseback on the first sighting, my grandfather never bothered chasing after him again. He figured the land had once belonged to him, and if he wanted to help my grandfather, who was half Native American, keep watch over it, that was fine with Jess.

In front of the library is a gorgeous bronze statue of Weatherford native Mary Martin sculpted by Ronald Thompson. Martin is famous for her role in *Peter Pan*. You must see it for yourself.

Also, you will see a marker noting the crash of two World War II bombers in the airspace above the library. It reads:

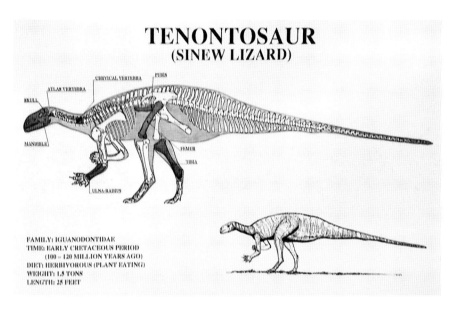

This page: Tenontosaur display, Weatherford Public Library.

On the night of August 17th, 1945, two B29 "heavy bombers" collided above this site, killing eighteen of the twenty airmen aboard. The spectacular event could be seen as far away as Gainesville, Greenville, and Cisco as both planes exploded in fire.

The two aircraft, one from Clovis Airfield, New Mexico, and the other from Alamogordo Airfield in New Mexico, were on separate training missions to simulate bomb runs in the Pacific as they met head-on in a freak chance over Weatherford. The Clovis plane with a crew of eleven

This page: Mary Martin *Peter Pan* bronze statue.

crashed approximately one and a half miles southwest of this site on the Edwards family farm. Two of the men managed to parachute from the burning plane and survived. The Alamogordo plane with a crew of nine crashed approximately two and a half miles north of this site near the highway with no survivors. In 2003, fifty-eight years after the crash, the marker was erected to honor the brave airmen who sacrificed while serving their country. May they rest in peace.

CHAPTER 6

THE BAKER MANSION

304 SOUTH LAMAR STREET

Five families have owned the enormous 6,840-square-foot Victorian mansion at the corner of Lamar Street and Columbia Street in Weatherford. Each has left imprinted memories of their families and lives on the beautiful walls. One family stands out from the rest, and all the hauntings in the home are thought to come from them.

John Daniel Baker and his wife, Alice Upshaw Baker, had no idea what would happen to them as they built the beautiful home to raise their four children, Charles, Harry, Mary, and Ethel. The youngest, Alice Ethel Baker, born on June 29, 1881, passed away on March 23, 1894, just before her thirteenth birthday.

John was born on March 23, 1848, and moved from Alabama to Weatherford at age twenty-three with little money. He changed his fortune by starting a mercantile business and hauling his goods to Granbury from Dallas on wagons. He left a legacy of honest dealings and being highly respected in Granbury and Weatherford, where he owned several businesses and was president of a local bank. He passed, according to a newspaper article, several days after suffering appendicitis rupture while supervising another of his store openings. Unfortunately, he never saw the Baker Mansion completed, as he died on April 2, 1899, and the house was completed in 1904.

I noticed while researching this piece that his daughter Ethel died on her father John's birthday, March 23, an unusual and sad occurrence. Ten years later, their son Harry was killed while on a business trip to Chicago, leaving daughter Mary as the sole surviving heir. Mary was born on December 26, 1891. She married Joseph Rumsey II and moved to Oklahoma City, Oklahoma, where she passed after living a long life of ninety-one years, dying on December 4, 1983.

Those who have encountered a male spirit on the property say Charles Baker haunts the old mansion. He was a buyer for the family business. In 1908, while on a buying trip for the stores, he was reported as having been seen leaving San Francisco en route to Seattle, where he was to order more goods for the stores. Sadly, he was never seen or heard from again. His family sent out search parties and offered a $5,000 reward for any information to help them find Charles. This was a lot of money in those days, but no witnesses ever came forward to claim it. This is a true mystery.

A first-edition poster came up for sale in March 2024 for $350; it reads as follows: "Offers a reward of $5,000.00 that will be paid by Harry Baker of Baker, Poston & Co., Weatherford, Texas for the body, dead or alive of Chas. R. Baker, last heard of March 9th, 1908, in San Francisco, Cal., and supposed to have gone to Seattle the following day." A picture of Charles R. Baker is provided with a description which states in part:

Age 29 years, height 6ft., weight about 150 lbs., hair light, eyes blue, sharp features, smooth-shaven. Has a very perceptible limp in walking, caused by rheumatism, affecting feet mostly. He is a constant sufferer of this disease. Has a scar on the first finger of the right hand caused by a severe glass cut. Holds finger in a crooked position. Dry-goods merchant by occupation. Well-versed in business matters generally. Very quiet and gentlemanly in demeanor. Not dissipated. The First National Bank of Weatherford, Texas, guarantees the payment of the above reward.

In 1936, Mary had her missing brother Charles officially declared dead after twenty-eight long years of waiting for his return or word of what happened to him on that fateful trip.

There are different theories about what the ghostly apparitions seen on the property may be searching for when they glide down the stairs or come up the front steps at the Baker Mansion. Some believe Charles is trying to make contact to give a clue as to where his body lies or information to solve his mysterious vanishing on that fateful business trip. Others believe it is possibly a residual haunting rather than intelligent, with poor Charles's imprinted energy carrying on his old routines around the property he frequented in life.

Baker Mansion.

What about the sounds of sobbing, cold spots, and feeling of being watched or touched? Is this Charles, or could it also be sweet Ethel, who died so young, trying to be noticed? Imprinted energy can also be an auditory phenomenon. I think people may have heard the heartbreaking cries of the mother, Alice, who lived in the home until her death. Alice, for me, would be the best candidate for the spirit heard sobbing throughout the mansion. She lived through the loss of her young daughter Ethel; the deaths of her son Harry and her beloved husband, John; and the unending heartbreak of not knowing what happened to her son Charles. Those cries from a grieving person could leave an imprint on the home.

A close friend of mine visited the mansion as a schoolmate of one of the families who lived there. She remembers one occasion while visiting when her friend took her up to see the turret area of the home. When my friend walked past the turret window, she saw, clear as day, a woman all in black staring out the window from a chair pulled up close to the windowsill. She seemed as solid in form as any living being. My friend thought it odd that she was dressed in such old-fashioned clothes, so after a few steps, she turned to say hello and ask about the woman's clothing. The woman was not there and had vanished in seconds. Was this the spirit of Alice keeping watch from the turret window, longing to see her son Charles returning home? That is another unknown.

The Baker family retained the house in Weatherford until 1942, when mother Alice Baker passed away on April 13, just two weeks before her eighty-seventh birthday.

I HAD A SIMILAR disappearance with one of my brothers, Scott. He went on a deep-sea fishing trip in Mexico alone, against everyone's wishes. He was last seen flashing money on the dock while trying to get on a bigger boat. We did not find a trace of him for fifteen years. We tried involving the police and calling hotels, hospitals, and anywhere else we thought he might be.

Several family members passed away, and each time, our renewed efforts to find him and notify him fell flat. He had always been close to the family and even extended family, calling and visiting frequently, never missing a holiday or special family occasion, so this behavior felt to us like foul play must have taken his life.

By an odd occurrence, we finally had someone in a town about four hours from our family home contact us, saying they believed they saw him assisting others at a homeless shelter. Hoping but not expecting much after all these years, we discovered he had passed away two months prior from brain cancer. He had been helping at the shelter for several years but had no memory of his family or parents. He did have a big healed gash on his head. We can only assume he was hit in the head and lost his memory. Somehow, his homing instinct led him back to where he had lived before the trip, not far from his birthplace. Sadly, he passed before we could see each other again in life. He was given a proper burial even as a John Doe. We held another service when placing his marker, embracing him back into his family again.

Chapter 7

Twisted Snifter

111 NORTH MAIN STREET
817-933-9705

The Twisted Snifter is a fantastic shop in Weatherford owned by Neil and Michelle Kennedy. The shop carries specialty liquor, craft beer, local wines, and spirits—and not just those on the shelf. They cater to specific needs and gifts or can help you find the perfect pairing for your dinner plans. Everyone I spoke with said they are so friendly; that may be why spirits linger among them.

The owners have had their fair share of supernatural experiences in the store. Michelle even experienced a physical phenomenon: feeling a hand on her back while alone in the store. Another encounter happened when the ghosts made sure to be noticed here. The building's front door is heavy, but it opened by itself.

Wanting to understand more about these experiences, the Kennedys had several investigative teams come in. Contact was made with a female entity who stated she had two children with her. They believe the woman may have died in a fire or some way by having her breathing or airway restricted. She also seems to shy away when the male ghost is present. She may not want her gentle soul and those of her children around when the male entity often sensed in the building is near. This may be why these ghosts are seen and felt at different times.

The male spirit is often experienced and seems to command attention in the building. Brad is the name most associated with this ghost, as people

Twisted Snifter boutique bottle shop.

have had it come to mind, or it has been spoken over sessions using tools to pick up EVP. Electronic voice phenomena is when sound and voices are recorded onto tapes, videocassettes, or other electronic devices but a physical person is not present to speak the words recorded. The recordings are spirits trying to communicate with us.

Brad probably does the physical or poltergeist manifestations of making a bottle fly off the shelf at owner Neil. A box of stacked wine by the front of the store simultaneously fell over for no reason on one occasion. This male ghost seems to challenge Neil. Spirits retain their personalities in death, good and bad. He may have been in charge of a business there at one time in the history of the building or might be a male entity with a big ego even in death and wants to feel he is still the male in charge in some way.

This lovely 1880s building was originally a saddle shop but has been many other things in its 224-year history, including a haberdashery shop selling clothing and notions, law offices, and more. Owner Michelle told me she notices the paranormal activity ramps up in their store when changes are made or there are workings outside the building like street repairs. This is one common thread in intelligent hauntings. Like living individuals, spirits are concerned about the homes and businesses they loved and cared for. When changes happen, it can upset them and bring about the only way they have to protest change and protect their space: poltergeist activity. These encounters include knocks on walls, objects thrown by unseen hands, furniture moving, and other physical occurrences.

Michelle also used the building next door at one time. She thinks the ghostly visitors may wander from building to building because she could hear chairs stored upstairs being dragged across the floor without explanation when she was working next door. Before Michelle was in that building, it had been a bookstore. They told her there were times they opened the store after it had been securely locked overnight to find books had been wiped off a shelf or placed in another location with no explanation of how these things could have happened.

Disembodied voices are ghostly voices you hear without devices or gadgets to help them occur or help you hear them. Both the owners have experienced this. Neil heard somebody call out distinctly to him, "Hey!" when nobody else was in the building. On a different occasion, Michelle heard the same "Hey!" called out to her when she was alone in the store.

My favorite ghostly happening Michelle told me about in the store was when children's handprints appeared inside a locked door with condensation dripping down from the pressure points of their tiny hands pressed against the glass. The store had not been opened yet, and no living children were inside to explain them. Were the little ghost children running to greet the owners as they opened the front door on that chilly day? The same children's handprints have also been seen on the store's chalkboard without anyone in the building physically making them.

One night, when Neil was in his office after closing the store, he saw shadows of feet passing underneath the closed door, blocking out the light shining through the crack beneath the door. There was no way anyone else was in the building. Maybe that was Brad, the male ghost, making his presence known, or it could have been the female spirit venturing out and checking on things.

Left: Twisted Snifter ghostly handprints. *Photo by Michelle Kennedy.*

Right: Front door with child's handprints. *Photo by Michelle Kennedy.*

Speaking of spirits making themselves known, while writing this story, I left the room and heard my dictation app beep. When I returned to see what had happened, I saw a sentence had been written at the end of the story. It said, "Okay, it's a goodie." Nobody alive was in the house besides me; there was no television or music to activate the mic. This accidental recording has never happened before or since. One of my resident ghosts must also like the Twisted Snifter story.

CHAPTER 8
APPARITIONS AT CHANDOR GARDENS

711 WEST LEE AVENUE
817-613-1700

*Adults five dollars each, children ages twelve and under free
but must be accompanied by an adult*

Chandor Gardens is said to be the heart of Weatherford's Historic District, blending the beauty of Chinese architecture with an elegant English formal garden. Generations of locals and visitors have stories about the beauty they see there and tales of restless spirits that wander the gardens.

Douglas Chandor, a British-born portrait artist, purchased Chandor Gardens, originally named White Shadows, in 1936. His widow, Ina, renamed it Chandor Gardens after Douglas's death in 1953, keeping it open to the public until she died in 1978. After Ina's passing, the gardens fell into neglect. Melody and Chuck Bradford revived them along with Chandor's house and studio, making them a place to tour and hold private parties or beautiful weddings. The City of Weatherford acquired the beautiful gardens in 2002.

Chandor was one of the great artists of his time. He added over three hundred paintings to his credit in his lifetime. Five of his most admired paintings were exhibited in the Smithsonian National Portrait Gallery. His works include Winston Churchill, President Franklin Roosevelt, Eleanor Roosevelt, President Herbert Hoover, and Sam Rayburn; his last picture was of Queen Elizabeth II.

Chandor did not start his life out as an artist. He was a soldier in World War I. Injured during the war, he revisited his childhood love of painting while recuperating. From this, his beautiful life as a painter blossomed. In 1921, he officially launched his artistic career with a portrait of the Prince of Wales. You can see some of Douglas Chandor's paintings in person at the Dallas Museum of Art. How did a British soldier turned artist end up in Weatherford, Texas? Well, he met his second wife there, and she and the beauty of Texas stole the Brit's heart.

Chandor came to love Texas and envisioned his gardens before ever building his house. It was his passion and not easily created. The land was caliche, hard as a rock; having used dynamite and determination, it yielded a lush beauty after sixteen laborious years.

There is a marker on the property that reads, "711 West Lee—Built in 1936. Listed in the National Register of Historic Places by the United States Department of the Interior."

A man's ghostly illuminated figure is said to appear wandering the property after the gates are locked. A shadowy figure has also been seen near the Moon Gate and in his studio during the day.

What makes such a beloved space supposedly haunted? Is it the tranquility once found visiting there? Or perhaps Chandor can't stay away from his much-loved work of art. We will never honestly know the answers, but a

Famous gardens of artist Douglas Chandor. *Postcard by Stryker's Western Fotocolor.*

woman in a white flowing gown has also been seen through the years gliding through the gardens, her features obscured by a veil of mist. Some claim to have felt an icy breeze caress their skin as she passed, while others have heard whispers they can't make out carried on the wind. Orbs, thought to be spirits expressed as balls of light, are reportedly seen most often at the ornate gates of the main entrance on Simmons Street. Could this be Chandor and his wife, Ina, reunited after their deaths? Or perhaps other spirits are enjoying the gardens; we will never know.

There is an unusual structure called the Moon Gate, which was built in 1949. The figures on top are thought to bring good luck. The current garden's site details describe it as having lipped tiles that give off different sounds as rainwater runs down them. They also invite you to be aware of the differing sounds of your voice as you pass through the unique Moon Gate. Could this account for some indistinguishable sounds drifting through the gardens sometimes?

The house and path were built in 1939. There's a path around the Chandor house with an island off the south porch. The home, designed by architect Joseph Pelich, was also added in the 1940s, and once again, additions were made after Chandor died in the 1950s.

The Ming bridge, which has a small dock, is to the left of the front door. Chandor kept a tiny boat secured at this spot. Farther down the path, you will see the house's side porch. A dragon figure on the south chimney over the porch faces the triple-tier fountain. The dragon's tail is shaped like a cloud, symbolizing good luck.

You will also see two toads kissing in the Cave Grotto area. An unofficial legend says that if you rub the toads' tummies for luck and place coins in their mouths, good fortune will come your way, and your wishes will come true. Hey, it's worth a try.

CHAPTER 9

RAILROAD GHOST STORIES

Since the late 1800s, stories have been told about unexplained lights seen traveling on and around the railroad tracks running through North Main Street in town. The lights sometimes seem to swing, as if the light source is a lantern held by an unseen hand. Some have reported seeing a person standing on the viaduct/bridge covering part of the railroad bridge's top. The reports differ on where he is standing, but he is always alone and holding something in his hands they can't make out.

That is as much information as anyone has ever given, so it's hard to figure out who the specter might be and from what era. He's always seen looking solid. Possibly, he is more of a shadow person, which are generally considered to be from the underworld or are dark entities with negative intentions. They differ from your typical ghost sighting. Ghosts are generally light in color and translucent in many descriptions. Shadow people are seldom translucent; they look more solid. They also appear in multiples or groups in some sightings. When they are encountered, they are almost always accompanied by a feeling of fear or danger, unlike ghost sightings, which sometimes make people more curious to find out who they are rather than instantly feel they are in danger.

Another story is of a figure seen standing on the tracks and then turning into a floating mist when approached to offer help in getting the person off the tracks. The sinister part of this tale is that the ghostly figure appears very solid in form at first, and then once it has lured the unsuspecting good citizen onto the dark tracks offering to help, it vanishes. When the mist clears, it's apparent that it has been blocking the approaching train's headlight, with the unsuspecting citizen narrowly escaping a horrible death on the very same tracks.

The earliest stories told match the current ones in circulation. Some believe the lights are the spirits of railway workers who met tragic ends during construction of the railroad that once ran through Veal's Station. Legend has it that two workers were killed in an accident, and their spirits wander the tracks. That may be true, but other, more sinister possibilities follow railroad history. Bandits and outlaws sometimes took lives along with goods and money.

There were three companies in the area, the first of which operated in Texas around 1853. In 1889, the Northwestern Railway Company was tasked with building twenty-five miles of track connecting Weatherford to Mineral Wells. The project was completed in 1891, and the line owned ninety cars and two locomotives to transport them along the new tracks. In 1902, the Texas and Pacific Railway Company bought the line and added eighteen miles from Mineral Wells to Graford by 1908. Later, an additional twelve miles of track were added, connecting Graford to Salesville. Finally, 1941 brought eight more miles of track between Mineral Wells and Salesville.

The Weatherford, Mineral Wells, and Northwestern Railroads were merged into the Missouri Pacific Railroad Company as successors to the Texas and Pacific Lines. By 1989, the line had been sold and then leased to Mineral Wells and the Eastern Railroad. Unfortunately, by 1992, the Mineral Wells and Eastern lines had closed down. With decades of railroad construction and closures, there have been plenty of deaths, murders, and even suicides to attribute to the lights and ghostly figures that surround the railroad's ghostly tales.

A historical marker reads:

> *Weatherford, Mineral Wells, and Northwestern Railway—In 1852, years before the nation's first transcontinental rail line was completed in 1869, the Texas Legislature chartered what would become the Texas & Pacific Railway Company. The Civil War halted progress, but in 1888, the line reached Weatherford in its advance westward to the Pacific Coast. The tracks then turned south to avoid the Palo Pinto Hills. This left northwestern Parker County and most of Palo Pinto County without rail support.*
>
> *In the 1880s, Mineral Wells became a resort. A stage line connected to the railroad at Millsap, but the town's popularity called for a rail*

connection. Several men led by W.A. Stone of Missouri received a charter for the Weatherford, Mineral Wells & Northwestern Railway Company in 1889. The line linked Mineral Wells to Weatherford, which by then was served by the T&P and Santa Fe railroads. They established a depot, offices, and repair shop in Weatherford. The new line, built largely on land obtained from the Franco-Texan Land Company, included stops at Lemley, Franco, Garner and Rock Creek. On January 1, 1891, a crowd in Mineral Wells greeted the first train's arrival, and in 1899 approximately 33,000 passengers made the trip each year from Weatherford to Mineral Wells. The line also supported freight shipments.

T&P eventually acquired the line and extended it to Salesville, Oran, and Graford. By the beginning of the 1940s, after decades of highway expansion, the rail line was no longer productive. The advent of World War II and the training of troops at nearby Camp Wolters resurrected the line briefly. It became part of the Missouri Pacific system in 1988 and closed in 1992.

CHAPTER 10

1908 Santa Fe Depot

401 FORT WORTH STREET

This 116-year-old pressed red brick building is a graceful beauty today. I can only imagine the fanfare it received when it opened its doors in 1908. The town went wild when the first, more modest station was built for the railroad, opening in the summer of 1880.

Having a railroad come through town meant everything, not only for commerce but also to provide a better quality of life for the town's residents. This created more jobs, faster delivery of goods, and the ability to travel faster, safer, and more comfortably than on horseback. Like many others, this town lost these things when the trains stopped running in 1959.

In the depot, the two arches above the entry doors and the four arches above the windows are made of stunning red bricks, making you feel like you are entering a special place. No wonder ghosts like it here.

The layout of the building was designed under the Jim Crow laws ordered in that era. Spaces within the building, by law, had to be built to divide men from women and also divide them by color. The space, when opened as a railroad station, consisted of three waiting rooms segregated by skin color and sex of the person, and these three rooms were divided by a ticket and telegraph office.

The original stationmaster's desk still stands where it was placed. Some say they have glimpsed his ghost, which is still working there. The brick loading platform remains intact, and I'm sure the Chamber of Commerce will keep this already well-preserved building at its best for many years to come, as they are its keeper now.

Other hauntings reported in the building are purposeful knockings on doors only to be met by empty rooms when answered. Sometimes, it feels playful to the living person. The knocking on doors takes them from room to room in the otherwise empty building. They don't feel exactly afraid but are very confused by it and happy to see other employees arrive for work.

Ghost stories flourished even when the train depot was still a bustling stopover on the way to the next destination. Unexplained lights on the tracks had to be investigated to ensure the safety of the riders and railroad workers. The same goes for sightings of a person standing on the tracks. There is no reasonable explanation for them, but they have persisted for over 140 years.

One of my most cherished ghost stories involves a young, possibly orphan boy who may have journeyed by train to or through Weatherford, searching for a new beginning. The story has been passed down through generations, and many believe in the existence of a little brown-haired boy ghost with the saddest blue eyes anyone has ever seen. The ghost is said to possess similar mannerisms and appearances across all accounts.

The little ghost boy appears only to young women while they wait for a train or loved ones to arrive. Suddenly, the woman finds herself in the company of a perhaps two-year-old boy sitting beside her. The story has captivated many due to the vivid details and eerie encounters shared over the years. He always wears a little gray jacket, even in warm weather, and short pants, tattered little brown shoes, and dark socks that have fallen to the tops of his shoes. He tugs on the woman's shirt or coat arm and gazes up with the most beautiful but sad blue eyes. He seems solid and fully formed until she reaches out to touch him, but at this point, he will vanish as if he had never been there. This has disturbed many young women because their hearts went out to this little child they felt needed help. They couldn't reconcile in their mind that he was a ghost. He seemed so solid, so how could he disappear in a flash? Some were frightened and left the building, but most ran around the benches and into the restrooms and other rooms, everywhere inside and outside the depot, searching for the boy because even though he had vanished before their eyes, he had to be a living boy. Their hearts couldn't accept other possibilities, even though their minds counseled otherwise.

Each account of this ghostly boy said he tugged on the woman's shirt or coat from the left side of their body—always the left. Each young woman asked the same question: How could he be a ghost? How could the little boy not be real? How could a ghost move their clothing?

In 1923, a woman heard the rustle of a sandwich she had in wax paper sitting to her left side on the bench. In the same instant, she heard his little voice say, "Help me," as he tugged her jacket. She found that the sandwich had not been bitten into, but the secured wrapper was open with the sandwich sitting on top. She distinctly felt a tug on her jacket that cold December evening. This story was entered in their family Bible. She could never shake the encounter and wanted it passed down through her family's history.

During the 1850s, many children lived on the streets of major cities and had to search for food and a warm, dry place to sleep. Some resourceful orphans managed to sell rags, matches, and newspapers to pay for food or a place to stay the night. It was a struggle to survive. The children formed gangs for protection because life on the streets was dangerous, and they were often victimized. Police would arrest these children, some as young as five years old, and put them in jail cells with adults. They seemed to have no one they could turn to for help.

In the late nineteenth century, the children began to be transported by trains to their new homes, and this program became known as the orphan trains. Charles Loring Brace, the founder of the Children's Aid Society, was the first to suggest placing children with families in the West instead of in orphanages. Orphanages were overcrowded and did not prepare children to become functioning adults who could care for themselves. Brace believed that families could help these children heal their broken hearts and that American pioneers settling in the West could use some help. He felt that this would be an arrangement that would make both sides happy.

Between 1900 and 1929, over five thousand children were brought to Texas through orphan trains. The last train arrived in Sulphur Springs, Texas. Most Catholic children from the New York Foundling Hospital came to Texas through New Orleans or Galveston and then traveled by ship and train to towns east and south of Houston, such as Victoria, Edna, Weimer, Schulenburg, and LaGrange. They settled primarily with Czech families. The Children's Aid Society also sent children who arrived by train through Texarkana and westward to towns between Texarkana and Wichita Falls. For instance, an orphan train rider in Austin, Texas, could have come from either one of these towns. People try to trace their roots to family members who may have been orphans and brought by train to one of these towns in the United States. There are more sources to pull from as records are added to online searchable records from many personal family accounts.

The orphan trains were ambitious and sometimes controversial rescue missions for poor and homeless children. They operated from 1854 to 1929 before the federal government became involved in child protection or welfare. Over 200,000 children were moved from cities like New York and Boston to the American West to be adopted and given a better chance at life.

Each organization had agents who visited communities several weeks before the placement of orphans. They advertised in newspapers and held meetings in various locations to ensure that as many people as possible knew the date the orphans would be coming to their town. Once the trains arrived with the orphans, adoptions were held at churches, hotels, schools, courthouses, theaters, or anywhere that could accommodate as many people as possible.

The children would typically arrive on a Friday. They would be cleaned up and given clean clothes to make them look their best. They would then be lined up on stage or in front of all the potential adopters at their best vantage point to be seen. The agent in charge would explain the mission of the Children's Aid Society and that each child was expected to be cared for by the foster parents as if it were a child born to them. They were told that these children were not their workers or kitchen helpers but must be sent to school and church to be instructed on becoming productive citizens.

One orphan, Rose, remembered being taught table manners, dressed in clean civilian clothes, and given two other outfits for her new life before she left her original home in Brooklyn. She and her brother were able to be adopted together in Missouri.

Beatrice Flanagan Polack Fojtik celebrated her 100th birthday in 2021 in Eagle Lake, Texas, before sadly passing away just two months later. She was one of the lucky ones. She had a full life and five children. She was known to be a fantastic seamstress and cook, even judging several contests. She is believed to be the last known living orphan train rider in the United States. She was born at New York's Bellevue Hospital. Her mother was a single Irish woman who worked as an elevator operator. She could not care for Beatrice and deposited the newborn at the front door of New York's Foundling Hospital. In 1922, when Beatrice turned fourteen months old, she was sent west on the orphan train.

The Texas State Historical Marker for the depot reads:

Built 1899. The Beaux Arts design features native stone banding. When intact, the north windows of painted glass depict travel from Pony Express to steam locomotives. Visitors here have included such world figures as Presidents Franklin D. Roosevelt, Dwight D. Eisenhower, and Lyndon B. Johnson. The depot was used by six railroad companies. As of 1970, Santa Fe served Texas with greater trackage than any other railroad, 5102 miles.

CHAPTER 11

WEATHERFORD SANITARIUM

Like many other sanitariums around the country, Weatherford Sanitarium has experienced ghostly shadows appearing on the walls or full-body apparitions crossing from one corridor to another or even walking through walls with soundless ease. Ghosts of people known to have died there of tuberculosis were seen staring back at the sanitarium from a grove of trees or even from the very doorways of rooms where their dead bodies had been taken from. Nothing remains of the towering structures, once beacons of hope in the battle against an unforgiving disease that spared no one, young or old.

Almost from the onset of the opening of the Weatherford Sanitarium, stories like these have passed through family folklore and are now being passed down to you. Unexplainable experiences were reported, such as hearing gurgling sounds and death rattles. These were heard by patients who recovered and lived everyday lives back home. They said that when somebody passed away, nurses and orderlies would shut the patient's doors on each side of the hall as the gurneys went down the hallway so patients weren't disturbed by hearing the sounds of gurgling and patients choking to death on their blood.

One man remembered being in his early teens when he had to go to the sanitarium for treatment. He would watch for feet and listen for the squeaking wheels of the gurneys underneath his door if it was shut, and if his door was open (which most of the time it was), he could better hear and count how many doors shut as orderlies took the body from the patient's room to the morgue or the operating room. By counting the doors closing, he believed he would know where the worst outbreaks were in the building in relation to the room he was staying in.

There have also been stories of screams, cries, moaning, doors closing, gurney wheels wiggling and squeaking from the weight of a body, and different sounds coming from the gurney without that weight. These stories came from people who worked at the sanitarium as well as patients.

Several of my family members had to spend time in this sanitarium and the sanitarium in San Angelo, Texas. Thankfully, they were two of the best operating in Texas at the time, but sadly, not all of them recovered. The nurses and doctors were said to be caring and skilled to the best level they could be trained in that era.

One of my young aunts, Mamie Lou, died of tuberculosis before her sixteenth birthday. She told our family that a young girl kept appearing by her bedside several weeks before she passed away. She would awaken with the girl standing beside the bed staring, never speaking. Mamie Lou felt like she was in the girl's bed and she should move. It disturbed her so much that she begged to come home. The family was worried her condition would worsen if they moved her, but when prayers, rosary beads, and crosses did not stop the ghostly visitations, they brought Mamie Lou home. She passed shortly after but was more at peace being in her bed and grateful that the ghost did not follow her home.

Weatherford Sanitarium. *Postcard by Gernsbacher Bros. Co.*

Something you don't read about but was happening at that time was the social repercussions of contracting the disease of tuberculosis, at the time referred to as consumption. Family members were shunned, and engagements were broken off. Many people thought that once infected, they would always be carriers of the disease. People did not want to bring consumption patients into their families or social clubs and even asked them to worship outside rather than sit inside the church service with other healthy members.

Being a nurse at the sanitarium took two years of training, and people had to have a genuine heart to enter this profession. Tuberculosis was a disease that had no cure. Treatments were sometimes more deadly than the disease. Germs were spread through the air. By the late 1800s, tuberculosis was a leading cause of death in the United States. It took many lives of all ages, and no one was safe from this airborne disease. Sadly, it is now back on the rise.

These sanitariums were what many would call isolation camps. They were generally set up in more remote areas and were self-contained cities. They held within their acres a chapel, a school, an area for plays and theater, and later, when available, a sitting area for listening to the radio or seeing a movie. There was a little general store where patients could buy stationery or personal items, snacks or sodas being the most desired and the costliest. Many wrote letters home asking for any money they could afford to be sent to treat themselves to something while recovering at the sanitarium.

These places had large dining rooms, where fresh air and sunlight were paramount to curing and preventing the spread of more germs. Most areas also had large open-air verandas or screened-in porches, as some might call them. These were not just for sitting and lying down to recover; many patients stayed there full time.

Some patients would sit on chairs backward entirely outdoors with a mirror attached to the back of the chair so that their mouths would open and the sunlight would reflect inside their mouths and throats. This treatment was intended to cure this part of their body. Sometimes, if not properly advised, it caused additional pain from sunburn on the tongue, mouth, and throat.

Different wings of the sanitarium held men separate from women, and aside from the adults, there were also wings for children that separated boys and girls. While the living spaces were ample to accommodate hundreds of people, a considerable waiting list seemed endless. The work these brave nurses and doctors did to assist in the healing of the patients was much appreciated by the patients and their families. There were never enough nurses or doctors to go around, and sometimes, one doctor would have to see several hundred patients as quickly as possible because there wasn't another doctor to assist.

Some children were brought by train and from the train station in trucks to the sanitarium from other areas farther away. These fresh-air children were meant to stay at the sanitarium for the summer months to get fresh air and healing treatments they couldn't get in their home locations. Upon arrival, they were checked for other diseases, and everyone was given a haircut. The haircut was for practicality rather than a uniform look, as many of the children would have lice. The short haircuts helped remove the lice and keep the area clean, making it easy for the nurses to inspect thoroughly. The children also got toothbrushes given to them for the duration of their stay. There were areas in the communal bathrooms where boxes of toothbrushing powder were mounted, and they would tap the powder onto their toothbrushes and use it. Everyone was responsible for keeping up with their personal items once issued.

When patients came to the sanitarium, they had to bring at least one pair of shoes and socks, and this was used throughout their time there; however, clothing was provided by the sanitarium. This way, the uniforms, if you want to call them that, were readily stocked and cleaned, sanitized, and handed out by size as best fitting as possible. Some wore what looked like big fabric diapers. This was so that when they exercised outside or lay in the sun for treatment, their bodies took in as much healing sunlight as possible. Fresh air, which you couldn't get in some congested cities, was considered the best medicine for the body.

Half a day of school was provided for children staying for the summer or those who were there as more permanent patients. During this schooling, lessons in core subjects were similar to or even more structured than they would have been outside the hospital.

Sewing classes for girls helped them learn the skill by starting with something simple they could accomplish, like baby doll dresses. Women also would sew to pass the time and make garments for themselves or their family and friends. The directors planned as many activities for the patients as possible. The nurses, orderlies, administration staff, and doctors wanted the best for their patients, so they tried everything possible to keep them comfortable and entertained during their stay at the sanitarium. I am sure the activities were a welcomed distraction for the patients from wondering about their fate while in care.

Milk was given twice a day and brought in from local farmers. This was considered one of the most helpful ways to keep the body healthy and fight deadly diseases. My grandmother Eula raised additional heads of red Guernsey milk cattle to donate to the sanitarium as a thank-you for saving all but one of her daughters sent there to recover. She said she raised this kind of cattle because they gave the best-tasting milk. I researched this and found that Guernsey milk contains 33 percent more vitamin D and 15 percent more calcium than average milk.

Long rows of sunbathing cloth covered the patient's heads while their bodies were exposed to the sun. The nurses and staff would have them turn over often to avoid burning their skin. They were very careful with the pale, delicate skin exposed to the hot Texas sun.

Unless patients were very ill, they were out every day of the year, hot or cold. This, of course, is why they were there, for this open-air healing. They were also expected to make their beds if they were capable. There was a daily inspection for the cleanliness of the body and the sheets on the bed. The patients' temperature was also taken daily to ensure no one had a fever. This was helpful for the nurses, as there were so many patients in relation to the number of nurses and staff. There were usually twenty beds in each room or section.

During the Christmas holidays, various organizations donated toys for the children, including baby dolls, jacks, cards, marbles, and anything else that might pass the time and help the children feel the joy of the season, even in this limited way.

Nurses lived in one wing of the buildings. Some wings housed huge laundry and sanitation wings, where clothes, bedding, and mattresses were sanitized. Staff lived in another section. Everyone working there lived according to their occupation, but married couples were allowed to live together in a wing or building separate from the others, who were already separated by gender and age group.

Often, cured patients became nurses and cared for those still recuperating after their two-year training. Many married orderlies, doctors, and workers lived their whole lives at the very place that cured them. Some histories passed down through families talked about patients wanting to become nurses and taking courses as they could. At the same time, they healed so that once well, they were not just starting on their two-year program but had already taken some active steps to become nurses as quickly as possible.

Thankfully, medical advancements in the 1950s made these facilities obsolete. The buildings shifted to asylums or other facilities or were torn down, and new hospitals replaced the old sanitariums. The old methods of treating patients now sound diabolical to our ears, but at the time, this was the best option the doctors and nurses knew about or were trained in to help heal the patients.

The old medical treatments were dangerous, sometimes requiring rib removal to reach the lungs. It was felt that if only one lung was infected, it should be put to rest to heal. To reach the lung, two or three ribs would be removed, and then several different methods would be used to collapse that lung, giving it, as they would say, "a rest." In some of the patients, these operations ended in death before they were even able to heal. For those who did survive the operation, the healing process was excruciating. Some patients had ping-pong balls—yes, you read that right—inserted into their collapsed lungs to help keep their shape and to let air pass around the balls, thinking this would help the lungs heal faster. Infections were rampant and difficult on the already ailing patients. Many died from infection, blood loss, or blood clots that weren't understood well at that time.

Another method used in the operating room that was thought to bring relief and healing involved removing part of the nerve running down the side of the neck. The doctors snipped the nerve and pulled it out with forceps like a piece of spaghetti. The patients who did live through these medical procedures spoke about the unimaginable pain they went through during the surgery, as well as the long road to healing that it often took. Looking back, we can see none of these procedures should have been done. But again, you have to think about what medical treatments were understood and the doctors' limited training in those days compared to modern times. They were doing the best they knew how to do at that time.

Unsurprisingly, patients and workers saw things they could not understand or explain throughout decades of being patients or working at the sanitarium. They knew they were surrounded by the possibility of death lying beside them or coming for them. Sometimes, it was taken for granted that the sounds of screaming, moaning, and crying and seeing a flash of a person running past were coming from real people. It was only alarming when the workers or nurses saw or heard these things in areas they thought were closed to be sanitized or for other reasons. Believing a patient had wandered in by mistake and needed help back to their bed, they would stop what they were doing and go in search, only to discover empty rooms. Running to windows and doors to see if they could find the lost person, they would find that no one was anywhere nearby to explain what they heard or saw.

Another thing to remember is that while these sanitariums were healing tuberculosis patients as their primary purpose, they were also seeing polio patients, and massage rooms were set up to work mainly with them. Old newspaper write-ups tell of townspeople who were not ill with tuberculosis but would come for care at the sanitariums for accidents they had been in. Many articles state that people who had been in train or automobile accidents and suffered injuries were taken to the sanitarium. People who had heart attacks or other ailments or diseases of all kinds were also treated at the sanitarium. Mentally ill patients were cared for here as well.

So, while they had a primary function, they were also a place of help and healing for all patients needing care.

CHAPTER 12

Old City Greenwood Cemetery

300 FRONT STREET

There are thirty-eight cemeteries in Weatherford. Most of them seem to have everyone resting in peace, and no ghost stories are attached to them—except for the following. According to the City of Weatherford government website, the official ownership of the Old City Greenwood Cemetery is unknown. Very few records exist between the age of it and the courthouse fires. The only way to be buried here now is with proof that you are a descendant of a family with space available in a family plot, or possibly if you are indigent. There are modern-day heroes with monuments to honor their memories throughout the cemetery, including those of founding families.

It is the most haunted site visited by people I know. It is also associated with 160 years of ghostly tales. The year 2024 marks 20 years that the Parker County Heritage Society hosts a tour here. As you walk through the cemetery, docents help some of the town's founders and famous people buried here come to life as they would have dressed and play out some scenes of their lives. This is always great fun.

When the cemetery opened, purchasing a plot for burial cost as little as five dollars. These days, you would need to add some zeroes to that. Historical markers are scattered throughout the gravestones to note important burials and the stories of those buried there. The first one you might encounter is upon entering the gate near 300 East Front Street. It reads:

This cemetery was formerly established by the Weatherford Town Council in 1863 when lots were surveyed and the exact cemetery location was staked. Previous interments were made in the unmarked streets of the town. The mayor directed those remains to be moved to the new cemetery.

Historian H. Smythe noted in 1877 that the cemetery was a "sadly neglected spot," without a fence. By 1925 the civic league and cemetery association had been formed. The accomplishments of its women members were many. In addition to site beautification, the driveways were widened and graveled. A water well and windmill were installed, and a sexton was employed to secure the grounds. Cemetery care declined in the 1930s and later.

Among the estimated 1,000 graves are Civil War Medal of Honor Recipient Chester Bowen; Trail Drivers Oliver Loving and Boze Ikard; Cattleman and founder of the Citizens National Bank J.R. Couts; Governor of Texas (1902–06) S.W.T. Lanham and his son, Congressman Fritz G. Lanham; veterans of many wars, and pioneers of early Texas history.

Restoration of the cemetery began in the late 1980s. The site continues to serve the area.

One interesting burial spot in this cemetery is the "Witches' Tomb." This is the most controversial burial story I know of in the cemetery and I think maybe any of the local cemeteries. It centers on a mausoleum. Visiting it for the first time years ago, I was surprised to see many presents left at an altar set up on the ledge of the tomb. Little tokens, candles, charms, rocks, crystals, and flowers were all lined up beside each other. All of these gifts were for the witch. If you knock on the door of this more-than-140-year-old mausoleum, it is said that you will hear a knock back. If you leave a token and ask for help, it will be given to you. People report hearing strange voices and even music. Strange lights are said to appear around the tomb at night. Shadows have been seen moving from the tomb along the tree line, as if the spirit was strolling through the rest of the cemetery. Many people believe that the witch is buried there, even though they know there is only a memorial note relating to Hiram E. Swain and his adopted daughter, Katie. Swain was a captain of whaling ships out of Belfast, Maine. He decided he wanted to move to the quiet of Weatherford. In 1878, he did just that with his second wife, Mary, and adopted a daughter, Katie. In 1883, Hiram E. Swain went to San Francisco, where he became ill and died at forty-seven years old. His body was returned to Weatherford for burial in the only crypt at the Old City Greenwood Cemetery. His daughter Katie was buried there with him one year later, in 1884. She passed away at the very young age of twelve, just five years after being adopted.

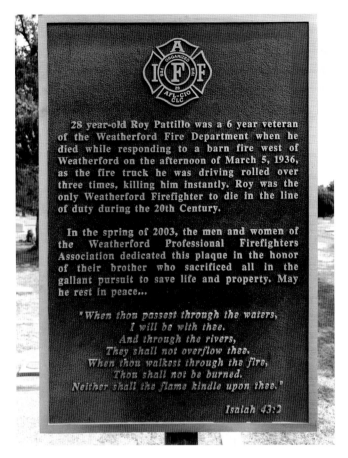

28 year-old Roy Pattillo was a 6 year veteran of the Weatherford Fire Department when he died while responding to a barn fire west of Weatherford on the afternoon of March 5, 1936, as the fire truck he was driving rolled over three times, killing him instantly. Roy was the only Weatherford Firefighter to die in the line of duty during the 20th Century.

In the spring of 2003, the men and women of the Weatherford Professional Firefighters Association dedicated this plaque in the honor of their brother who sacrificed all in the gallant pursuit to save life and property. May he rest in peace...

"When thou passest through the waters,
I will be with thee.
And through the rivers,
They shall not overflow thee.
When thou walkest through the fire,
Thou shall not be burned.
Neither shall the flame kindle upon thee."

Isaiah 43:2

Marker for fireman Roy Pattillo in City Greenwood Cemetery.

There used to be an iron doorway into the crypt. When I visited a few months ago, there were still pieces of the iron fence on the sides of the crypt. People believe that the witch is associated with this grave somehow. Is she illegally buried either beside the crypt or on the land right as you enter? As far as I know, officials have never checked to see if a woman's body was buried there without permission. Nefarious things happen in cemeteries in the dead of night.

There are two sides with definite ideas about this. Some don't care what anyone says. They believe they've had wishes granted, felt her presence, and seen the witch themselves coming out of her crypt to roam the cemetery. Then there are those who, despite having seen things they can't explain, will never believe this story, and they believe that only Hiram and his adopted daughter Katie rest there. You make up your own mind. But it wouldn't hurt to place a rock or some flowers

Left: "Witches' Tomb" in Old City Greenwood Cemetery.

Below: Swain family memorial on "Witches' Tomb."

there just in case respect needs to be paid to more than just those buried within the crypt.

Cattle drover Oliver Loving's life story inspired Texas author Larry McMurtry's bestselling novel and hit made-for-television series *Lonesome Dove*. His Texas State Historical Marker, on the Front Street side of this cemetery, reads:

> *The Dean of Texas Trail Drivers Oliver Loving (1812–1867). Founder of three major cattle trails, Oliver Loving came from Kentucky to Texas in 1845 and to Parker County about 1855. During the Civil War (1861–65), he supplied beef to Confederate forces. With Charles Goodnight as partner on a drive to New Mexico, Loving scouted ahead of the cattle, was badly wounded by Indians, lay five days without food before his rescue, and died of gangrene on September 25, 1867. His dying wish was fulfilled when his son Joseph joined Goodnight to bring the body 600 miles by wagon for burial in this county.*

Oliver was killed by Indians in New Mexico in 1867. His dying wish to his dear friend Charles Goodnight was not to leave him there but to bring his body back home. Charles kept his promise to his dying friend, making a very difficult journey over six hundred miles from the attack in New Mexico to bury Oliver in Old City Greenwood Cemetery. The historical marker in the cemetery reads, "A year before this, Goodnight had invented the first chuckwagon, which catered to cowboys on a cattle drive that would later be known as the Goodnight-Loving Trail. Bose Ikard, who served with Goodnight and was the model for the McMurtry character 'Deets,' was also laid to rest in Greenwood Cemetery."

Bose Ikard's Texas State Historical Marker is located on the west side of the Old City Greenwood Cemetery. It reads:

> *Born a slave in Mississippi, Bose Ikard came to Texas as a child with the family of his owner, Dr. Milton L. Ikard. He remained as an employee of Dr. Ikard following his emancipation, but in 1866 joined a cattle drive to Colorado led by Charles Goodnight and Oliver Loving. Ikard became one of Goodnight's best cowboys and a trusted friend. Following his work in the cattle drives, Ikard settled in Weatherford. He and his wife Angeline were the parents of six children. When he died in 1929 at age 85, Goodnight had a granite marker erected at his grave.*

Left: Historical marker for Oliver Loving.

Opposite: City Greenwood Cemetery.

Some notable graves and markers are sprinkled throughout the cemetery. One, located at the intersection of East Water Street and North Rusk Street, is for James Robertson Couts (1833–1904). A native of Tennessee and a veteran of the Civil War, Couts brought his family to Parker County in the mid-1860s. With proceeds from a cattle drive to California, he opened a bank in Weatherford (now Citizens National Bank). An influential citizen of the town, he left an endowment to Weatherford College in his will. Married twice, Couts was the father of six children. He is buried here next to his first wife, Martha.

Another grave often visited is that of Samuel Redgate, who came with Stephen F. Austin and three hundred other original settlers to the wilds of Texas. His marker reads:

> *Samuel Joseph Redgate—Born in England, 1800 Member of Legislature, 1858–1861. Died May 20, 1893. Jane Yergins Jordt, Daughter of Mr. and Mrs. Yergins, Wife of H.E. Jordt, was born in what is now Oklahoma on August 20, 1836, and Died on April 8, 1896. In Memory of Mary Yergins-Redgate. Born in Germany on June 11, 1816, Died in Dayton,*

Ohio, on October 31, 1881. Shortly after Indians captured Mrs. Yergins in 1836, a daughter, Jane, was born, and the two were ransomed. Mrs. Yergins, after the death of her husband, was married to Samuel J. Redgate.

While every life lived and lost has its tale, one of the most famous legends from Greenwood Cemetery involves the ghost of a young woman named Emily. According to local lore, Emily was tragically murdered by a jealous lover in the late 1800s. Visitors see a misty figure in a flowing white dress, believed to be Emily, wandering among the tombstones. Some even claim to have heard her soft sobs echoing through the night.

A wake of vultures at City Greenwood Cemetery.

Another ghostly tale is of the apparition of a Confederate soldier forever lingering near his grave. It is said that he met his untimely demise during the Civil War and has remained here, unable to find peace. Witness accounts describe a figure in a tattered gray uniform, silently patrolling the cemetery as if eternally guarding his resting place.

But it's not just human spirits that are said to haunt Greenwood Cemetery. Some ghost seekers have reported encountering the spirit of a loyal canine companion that is said to have been buried alongside his beloved owner. Visitors have shared stories of feeling a cold nose nudge against their hand and hearing the faint sound of paws trotting on the paths between the graves.

CHAPTER 13

CLARK CEMETERY

6401 OLD SPRINGTOWN ROAD

Clark Cemetery was established over 160 years ago. There are memorial records for 480 souls buried here. The oldest burial known in this cemetery is that of Anzaline "Anzelina" Barker Godfrey, born in Missouri on January 10, 1831, and died on February 4, 1859, at age twenty-eight.

This cemetery has many noted people resting here. The ghost stories from this cemetery differ from others in that they are centered on seeing not individual ghosts but a group of what appear to be five women carrying baskets of flowers, what look like small hand tools for cleaning the grave sites, and a quilt. Possibly in life, these ladies met and took care of their loved ones' graves or the cemetery in general. Some of the stories say they heard a group of voices humming. Others did not hear the humming of the group but saw the ladies all with their heads covered with sunbonnets and wearing old-fashioned clothes, and several looked to have aprons on as well. At first, they seem to be real, solid people before disappearing slowly, from solid to see-through, evaporating in groups of two or three. They never disappear one at a time or all at once. Those who thought of themselves as lucky to see them felt moved to see these women who were there making sure the ones they love are cared for. This could be a residual haunting, as they have never interacted with or acknowledged the onlookers. It could be the image of the time they spent their replays on a loop, or maybe they are intelligent hauntings and are just minding their own business. Seeing this group has made some feel comforted to know there is a part of us that lives on, still caring for others. I am comforted by this group of ladies as well. As I am a quilter, I always asked the people I interviewed if they remembered any details about the quilt. They recalled that it was made of colorful squares without a specific pattern. One person was also a quilter who collected antique quilts and picked up on some of the squares, which reminded them of the old flour sacks made into clothes or quilts after their usefulness as a container for flour or feed was completed.

The Texas Historic Cemetery Marker reads:

A common burial ground for early pioneer settlers who camped along the Clear Fork of the Trinity River, the Clark Cemetery consists of many burial sites from the 1830s. In December of 1853, Reverend John William Godfrey (1825–1897) and his wife, Anzaline (Barker) Godfrey (1831–1859), arrived in Parker County from Missouri. Godfrey established a Methodist Church in the Wright Community, northeast of Weatherford, where they lived. In 1859, Anzaline passed away and was buried in the Wright Community burial grounds. In 1880, Jim Clark and William Henry Ward formally established a permanent cemetery at the original location of Godfrey's Chapel Methodist Church. In 1953, signed documents deeded tract no. 1 and no. 2 of the land as burial plot property. Additional land was added in 1958 and in 1999.

In addition to numerous pioneer families and farmers, Clark Cemetery is the final resting place of a founder of early Parker County Methodist Churches, an organizer of Jack County, a trustee of an early pioneer school and a county chief justice. The oldest marked headstone in the cemetery belongs to Anzaline Godfrey, although sixty-five unidentified burial sites from the pioneer era were discovered with ground penetrating radar. The connection to military service is represented by veterans of the Texas Rangers, the Civil War, World War I, World War II, Vietnam and the Korean War. The landscape of the Clark Cemetery is traditional with live oak, elm and post oak trees with a limestone and steel entrance gate, restrooms and a covered pavilion. The Clark Cemetery Association continues to care for this historic cemetery.

CHAPTER 14

BAKER CEMETERY

In 1854, Josiah and Nancy Catherine "Kate" Baker and their four children, Josiah's parents, and Kate's mother settled in an area later known as Baker. The community grew around their homestead, and in the early days, a cotton gin and a general store were added. In 1872, the Bakers donated a portion of their land to establish a school that served the educational needs of the children in the area until it was merged with the schools in Weatherford in the 1950s. Josiah and Kate Baker also donated the land to construct Baker Baptist Church. Elizabeth, Josiah Baker's mother, passed away in 1854 and was buried in what is now known as the Baker Cemetery. Her burial is the first documented in the cemetery.

My grandmother Eula's maiden name was Baker, and upon checking genealogy records, I found connections to some of the Bakers buried in this now-abandoned cemetery. Some of my relatives remember her visiting them and talking about stopping by to clean some of the graves and bringing flowers to plant in this cemetery when she visited from Victoria and Lolita, Texas. They also shared ghost stories.

Apparently, local and visiting relatives had caught glimpses of little children who seemed to come in and out of focus into our dimension from the other side. Their giggles were almost always heard before they were seen in the cemetery. Thinking other families were walking in, my relatives would stand and look to greet them, but they would find nothing waving back except tall prairie grass. Some tried to shake it off as an odd bird song or nearby but unseen horse whinnies. But I remember my mother saying that when she was old enough and allowed to go with her mother, Eula, to tend the graves, she was warned to watch for snakes and sinkhole graves and not to go off chasing children she thought she saw. "They are just ghosts, and we don't mess with that," she recalled.

Baker Cemetery is just five miles from Spring Creek Cemetery. The Abandoned Cemetery Association of Parker County, Inc., restores and maintains this cemetery, established in 1854, with forty-nine headstones. A Texas Historical Marker one-third mile south of the cemetery at the Baker Baptist Church, 1912 Baker Cut Off Road, reads:

> Settlement in this part of Parker County began in earnest in the 1850s, and the county was formally established in 1855. Josiah and Nancy Catherine "Kate" Baker, their four children, Josiah's parents, and Kate's mother came to this area in 1854. The community that grew up around their homestead came to be called Baker. A general store and cotton gin were early commercial ventures.
>
> The Bakers donated land for the community school, which began in 1872 and was designated Baker School District No. 60 in 1884. It served the educational needs of children in the area until it was consolidated with Weatherford Schools in the 1950s. Josiah and Kate Baker also gave the land for Baker Baptist Church, which prominent pioneer Baptist minister Noah T. Byars organized as Shiloh Missionary Baptist Church in 1854.
>
> Josiah Baker's mother, Elizabeth, died in 1854 and was buried in what became the Baker Cemetery. Hers is the first documented burial in the cemetery, the resting place of Josiah's father, Martin (d. 1858), and his wife, Kate (d. 1895). A Civil War veteran, Josiah moved from the community in 1895 and was buried in Crystal Falls in nearby Stephens County upon his death in 1907.
>
> As a pioneer community in this state region, Baker is a part of the rural heritage of Parker County and of Texas. It is a reminder of early settlement patterns as pioneers came to this area and made their homes.

CHAPTER 15
SPRING CREEK CEMETERY

100 SPRING CREEK ROAD

This cemetery has 857 headstones. The Texas Historical Commission marker for the Spring Creek Community tells of the area's settlement.

> *Beginning in 1854, with the arrival of the T.J. Shaw family from Tennessee. They built a log cabin on the south branch of Spring Creek, and the community was built up in the area and named for the creek.*
>
> *As more settlers arrived, the community grew to include many homes and farms. Jeff W. Pittillo came in 1855, and he and his family eventually donated land to the community for a school, church, and cemetery. In 1856, A.L. Pickard brought his family and three slave families to the Spring Creek area.*
>
> *Congregations of the Methodist, Baptist, and Cumberland Presbyterian Churches were formed. A Tabernacle (Built in 1914 from a 1904 Brush Arbor) and a 1917 Schoolhouse remain in the community.*
>
> *The Spring Creek Cemetery contains the graves of many Pioneers from many areas. The earliest documented burial, that of Humphrey Price, dates to 1856. Also included among the burials are many unmarked graves and interments of slave families. Descendants of many Spring Creek Pioneer families still reside in the vicinity.*

There is another historical marker in the northeast corner of the cemetery. It reads, "Colonel Alfred G. Cooper—Seminole Florida War, 1836. Captain in Mexican War, 1846. Lt. Colonel Confederate Army, 1862. Born in Tennessee, June 22, 1817. Died February 28, 1883."

There have been reports of hauntings in this cemetery, but of a compassionate nature. Visitors have reported feeling an icy hand on their arm or elbow while walking through or bending down to look at a grave, as if someone is trying to help them up. Another type of encounter involves seeing a man in old-fashioned clothing standing off to the side at the very back of the cemetery. If people are coming from the front or more toward the center or the back of the cemetery, they see this figure toward the front, simply observing them. However, nobody has ever been bothered by this spirit. He seems to be a watchful guardian of the cemetery, ensuring that everything is respected and as it should be.

CHAPTER 16
HOGGARD-REYNOLDS CEMETERY

777 SOUTH STEWART STREET, AZLE

This cemetery sits eighteen miles from Spring Creek Cemetery. I love this cemetery and its history. During a time when so many people were fighting each other, the heart of Sarah to give a plot of her land to bury an African American child, Francis Reynolds, who died while traveling through the area is just such a touching story. She had the heart to do the right thing even though she did not know the pioneers traveling through.

This marker reads, "Hoggard-Reynolds Cemetery First burial. This exact spot is the resting place of a little black boy who died while traveling through the area with his family following the Civil War in 1865. Sarah Fletcher Hoggard allowed him to be buried here after local cemeteries denied him burial."

This cemetery is easy to reach, and there were excellent gravel roads when I visited. There have always been stories of unexplained humming at this location, like someone humming a song in this cemetery and down the gravel road beyond it. I know people who claim to have heard this on more than one occasion. Some believe these are spirits of past family members humming while they buried their dead here or perhaps tending the graves. Others can't explain what appear to be lights. They find them fascinating. I came out twice and never saw any lights or orbs or felt anything unusual. I understand that sometimes, in more remote and quiet areas, different things may be picked up by more receptive people. So, when you come to pay your respects, keep your eyes open for those mysterious lights and listen for the sounds of someone humming.

The historical marker reads:

According to oral history, pioneer farmer and Confederate widow Sarah Hoggard gave a plot of her land for the burial of an African American child who died while traveling through the area with his family after the Civil War. Though there may be earlier graves, the first marked burial on this site is that of Francis Reynolds, who died in 1865. Sarah and James Hoggard's daughter Matilda married Benjamin Reynolds, whose father operated the first cotton gin and grist mill in the area, and his family name became as prominent among the graves as that of the Hoggards. In 1899, the "Hoggard Graveyard" was set aside in a deed on the Hoggard family land. Reynolds was formally added to the cemetery name in 1984 after Reynolds descendant deeded additional land. The cemetery is a chronicle of area pioneers.

CHAPTER 17
OAKLAND CEMETERY

MILL AND BRIDGE STREETS

This cemetery is east of City Greenwood Cemetery. East Greenwood and Oakland run side by side. Oakland has no sign, and East Greenwood has one sign, and there is no fence between Oakland and it. There are 3,997 recorded burials here.

This is a peaceful cemetery to me. There is a feeling of stepping back in time when visiting here. One legend tells of a baby that can be heard crying. People have told me that they were in the cemetery to take pictures at different times of day and early evening, practicing their new hobby of photography. No one else was around, and they heard a baby crying. This was no place to abandon a baby. Animals would carry it off for sure. They were so disturbed by the cries that they enlisted three friends to help them search. When the friends arrived, everything was quiet. Then, after they searched everywhere and were about to leave, the cries started again. They called and reported the cries and felt foolish after someone the friends knew told them this had been happening for over fifty years in the cemetery. It always gets searched because you have to take seriously any cry from a baby or child to be sure they are not hurt or abandoned. So, if you visit and find yourself alone in the cemetery, you might hear a baby crying. Of course, babies are buried here, but I found no records of unusual burials or life details that could shed any light on this mystery baby.

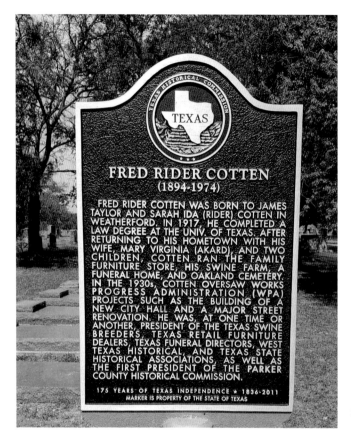

FRED RIDER COTTEN
(1894-1974)

FRED RIDER COTTEN WAS BORN TO JAMES TAYLOR AND SARAH IDA (RIDER) COTTEN IN WEATHERFORD. IN 1917, HE COMPLETED A LAW DEGREE AT THE UNIV. OF TEXAS. AFTER RETURNING TO HIS HOMETOWN WITH HIS WIFE, MARY VIRGINIA (AKARD), AND TWO CHILDREN, COTTEN RAN THE FAMILY FURNITURE STORE, HIS SWINE FARM, A FUNERAL HOME, AND OAKLAND CEMETERY. IN THE 1930s, COTTEN OVERSAW WORKS PROGRESS ADMINISTRATION (WPA) PROJECTS SUCH AS THE BUILDING OF A NEW CITY HALL AND A MAJOR STREET RENOVATION. HE WAS, AT ONE TIME OR ANOTHER, PRESIDENT OF THE TEXAS SWINE BREEDERS, TEXAS RETAIL FURNITURE DEALERS, TEXAS FUNERAL DIRECTORS, WEST TEXAS HISTORICAL, AND TEXAS STATE HISTORICAL ASSOCIATIONS, AS WELL AS THE FIRST PRESIDENT OF THE PARKER COUNTY HISTORICAL COMMISSION.

175 YEARS OF TEXAS INDEPENDENCE ★ 1836-2011
MARKER IS PROPERTY OF THE STATE OF TEXAS

Historical marker for Fred Rider Cotten.

The Lions Club International plaque at the grave of R. Roy Keaton says:

R. Roy Keaton, a Weatherford native, became Special Representative for Lions Clubs International in 1934, establishing Lions Clubs across the United States, Mexico, and Canada. Roy was named Assistant Secretary General in 1945 and heir apparent to succeed Melvin Jones, the Founder of Lionism. In 1948, Roy Keaton was named Director General becoming head of the world's largest service organization. Under his leadership, Lions Clubs membership increased from 380,000 members to more than 600,000 Lions and the scope of Lionism spread from 28 to 102 countries. In 2000 there are more than 1.4 million Lions Clubs members in 185 countries and geographic locations. The unprecedented growth of Lions Clubs was largely because of the dynamic leadership, vision and tireless efforts of Robert Roy Keaton.

A Texas State Historical Marker located on North Mill Street for Fred Rider Cotten (1894–1974) reads:

> *Fred Rider Cotten was born to James Taylor and Sarah Ida (Rider) Cotten in Weatherford. In 1917, he completed a law degree at the Univ. of Texas. After returning to his hometown with his wife, Mary Virginia (Akard), and two children, Cotten ran the family furniture store, his swine farm, a funeral home, and Oakland Cemetery. In the 1930s, Cotten oversaw Works Progress Administration (WPA) projects such as the building of a new city hall and a major street renovation. He was, at one time or another, president of the Texas Swine Breeders, Texas Retail Furniture Dealers, Texas Funeral Directors, West Texas Historical, and Texas State Historical Associations, as well as the first president of the Parker County Historical Commission.*

Another important figure to Weatherford buried here is Gustavus Adolphus Holland (January 12, 1859–March 11, 1946). His marker can be found at the intersection of North Mill Street and Estel Street. A teacher in his native Kentucky, G.A. Holland came to Parker County in 1882, settling in Poolville. In addition to teaching school, Holland served as postmaster and justice of the peace. He later served as county tax collector, Weatherford school board member, president of Citizens National Bank, and mayor of Weatherford. He published a history of Parker County in the 1930s. Married to the former Genareo Wynn, Holland was the father of six children.

CHAPTER 18

THE PHANTOM STAGECOACH

T he legend of the phantom stagecoach dates back to the late 1800s, when the stagecoach was a common mode of transportation in Weatherford. Many encounters with the ghostly stagecoach have been reported over the years. According to local folklore, the stagecoach appears late at night or before dawn, galloping down the historic downtown streets as if pulled by invisible horses. Witnesses have reported hearing thunderous hoofbeats and wooden wheels creaking and have even jumped back out of the road, believing it was a real horse-drawn wagon or coach as the ethereal vehicle passed them. The ghostly figure of a driver dressed in a long coat flowing in the wind and a wide-brimmed hat pulled down covering his face is also said to be seen. Some have even claimed to feel a chilling sensation of being watched as the stagecoach passes, leaving them with the unshakable feeling that they have had a supernatural experience.

As crazy as these legends sound in modern times, they endure. The phantom stagecoach has been seen on the old back roads of the town, and some farmers out before dawn have heard it. Some have seen what they describe as a faint shadow of it fading in and out in the few seconds it was visible to them.

I had an odd experience crossing the street in the historic downtown square of Denton, Texas. I was with a law enforcement friend late one night after leaving my haunted office on the second floor of the old opera house building. We both heard the sound of horses neighing, hooves, and wagon wheels creaking. At first, I was excited, thinking a company was bringing in carriage rides because I never understood why we don't have them here. We spun in all directions, looking for the source of the growing sounds surrounding us. We heard a man close beside us yell, "Hey!" Then silence took the place of all the swirling sounds. We looked at each other in disbelief. We heard the man call out and the phantom wagon and horses. I was new to the square and did not know about the stables that once stood there. We experienced possibly a residual playback or portal to the bustling times of old Denton. Maybe we even heard stablehand Sam Bass telling us to move out of the way as he and the Denton mare raced past. This stands as one of my most chilling and unexplained experiences. We still can't explain it.

CHAPTER 19

1869 MASON-BUILT WEATHERFORD COLLEGE

225 COLLEGE PARK DRIVE

The college in Weatherford is known for its rich history and even a ghostly past student, the lady in white, whom students and faculty have encountered.

Weatherford College has a rich history that dates back to 1869. As the oldest continuously operating community college in the Southwest, it has served the counties of Parker, Wise, Hood, Palo Pinto, and Jack for 155 years. The Phoenix Masonic Lodge was vital in leading the college's early years. The first structure was a two-story, seventy-five-by-fifty-foot building known as the Weatherford Masonic Institute.

However, the college faced financial problems for the first twenty years, which led to the sale of the Masonic Institute to M.C. Brown and its lease to the Methodist Church in 1885. At this point, the college was renamed Cleveland College, with hopes that President Grover Cleveland would provide support. Unfortunately, his support amounted only to one thousand copies of the congressional record.

In 1873, the Weatherford district conference of the Methodist Episcopal Church South passed a resolution to form a high school for Granbury. They erected a three-story stone building to house the school, but it faced financial problems. As a result, they decided to add junior college courses to increase revenue, and Granbury College began in 1881. The people of Granbury embraced the only Methodist junior college in West Texas, and the college grew in the next few years. However, a devastating fire destroyed the main building and all its contents. The college immediately initiated a rebuilding program, but with severe droughts, funds were unavailable. So, the college looked for a new home.

Eventually, the college found a new home in Weatherford, Texas. The Weatherford property was available for sale as Brown had been unable to make payments on his note for Cleveland College, and it reverted to the Phoenix Lodge. The citizen committee used its influence to move Granbury College to Weatherford. The citizens of Granbury complied with his request to provide the funds needed, and the Weatherford District Conference of the Methodist Church purchased the property, changing the name from Cleveland College to Weatherford College.

Weatherford College was a Methodist college from 1889 until 1901, when it was officially called Weatherford College Training School for Boys. Later, upon the admission of girls, the name was changed to Weatherford College Training School in 1921. The college was reorganized and became a junior college, offering college transfer courses again. In 1943, Weatherford College was merged with Southwestern University in Georgetown. However, this was short-lived, and Weatherford College was released to Parker County in 1949.

The lady in white is an enduring tale and is believed to be the ghost of a former student who met a tragic end on the college grounds. The circumstances surrounding her death vary from one account to another, adding to the mystery that surrounds her. Some say she suffered a broken heart and took her own life, while others believe she was a victim of foul play.

Witnesses have reported encountering the lady in white near the college's historic administration building, where she is often seen wandering the corridors or gazing out the windows. Her ghostly figure, dressed in a flowing white gown, emits an eerie glow that sends chills down the spines of those fortunate enough (or unfortunate enough) to witness her presence.

Several past students told me that they saw her on two occasions. One stormy late afternoon before the library closed, while going from a study room to various bookshelves in the library, they saw a flash of white out of the corners of their eyes. They passed it off as a student walking quickly between rows of books. But they saw it again for just a few seconds—the misty outline of a woman from the top of her head to just past her shoulders. It just dissipated from that mist to vanishing before their eyes.

This is a tale from when the original campus on South Main Street was near the historic downtown area before the new ninety-acre college campus was opened in 1968. Maintenance workers would hear an odd tapping noise against the windows, not so much the sound of fingernails as a small pebble

Weatherford College. *E.C. Kropp Co. Postcard.*

being gently thrown. The workers chalked it up to pranks being played by students or even rowdy youth who would roam around town bored and getting into trouble. The older male workers didn't seem to be as much the target as the new young man, who was more of a janitor who maintained pipes and boilers in that area. When the young janitor was mopping the floors and cleaning up in the science building, the tapping would happen and seem to follow him through different areas. He reported the odd occurrences to the head maintenance man, only to be told it was just pranksters and not to bother him with trivial matters like that again. This was said to continue for several weeks until one night, working alone in the building, the tapping started. The janitor was afraid but wouldn't risk being fired if he told his boss or the other workers the odd occurrences were still happening. So, he kept emptying trash baskets and mopping and straightening chairs and tables, making everything tidy for the next day's classes, as was his job description. The sound of pebbles became the tossing of pebbles at his feet as he cleaned. The temperature in the room dropped, and it is said that when he looked up from his work toward the dark doorway, only a few feet away, he saw a woman formed mainly by mist rather than flesh and bones standing and smiling at him. Laughter echoed as the figure vanished. He ran in the other direction, even though it was said to be the long way out of the building, hoping to get away from the impossible-to-believe experience he just had with the lady in white.

Stories of encounters with the lady in white have been whispered throughout the generations, so keep your senses sharp as you navigate Weatherford College's haunted grounds. The lady in white awaits.

CHAPTER 20
CAMPBELL HOSPITAL

713 EAST ANDERSON STREET

Campbell Hospital exuded an eerie energy when it closed as a hospital. The building now houses administrative offices for different businesses. Many ghost stories have emerged from its days as a hospital, and it's not hard to see why. People's experiences of fear and sadness seem to linger in the air, as do feelings of immense gratitude and joy.

Despite its being off-limits, people have entered the abandoned hospital over the years and found equipment still inside, such as gurneys, wheelchairs, and tables. It's almost as if everyone got up and left one day, never to return, leaving everything behind.

People have claimed to have encountered paranormal activity within the building. Unexplained banging sounds, footsteps shuffling down the hall, and doors opening and closing have been reported. The people I spoke with said the sound of shuffling feet following them was the creepiest feeling. Visitors have even heard loud noises, as if furniture was being dragged down the halls, only to find everything exactly as it was before. Unexplained voices whispering and yelling at them to leave have also been experienced.

The building has a long history of ghost stories, with people reporting sightings of full-body apparitions and sinister shadow figures crawling up the walls. If you remember, in the railroad stories, the shadow people or dark figures felt evil and like something not to be messed with by the experiencers. The same distinction applies here. While all the encounters are scary, the shadow figures crawling up the walls top the fear charts.

The scent of flowers has been reported to permeate the hospital's air despite nothing in bloom outside. Along with this came feelings of happiness even though they were surrounded by an empty, abandoned building without power, leaving a narrow flashlight view of everything around them. I am sure this would be creepy even before a paranormal encounter.

One paranormal experience I could do without that was heard here is the sound of a baby crying. Of course, the cries were immediately followed, and nothing was found anywhere in the building or the grounds. About thirty minutes later, after those having the experience had collected their nerves back inside the building, the cries were heard again, only louder and closer this time. Everyone knew it was time to leave. Cries and sightings of infants and children are sometimes dark spirits trying to lead a person into a dangerous space or situation or even trying to gain your trust in repeat situations where people use Ouija boards or devices to connect with the unseen world. I always caution people to use the methods only if they are well educated in protecting themselves against paranormal attacks that can happen.

My friend was born in this hospital in the 1980s, and ghost stories were already circulating then. Even after all these years, Campbell Hospital remains a place of mystery. It has a Texas Historical Marker that reads:

In the early twentieth century, medical care in Parker County was restricted to practices of individual doctors. That changed in 1924, when Dr. E.D. Fyke purchased the twenty-eight room G.M. Bowie family home in the 600 block of North Main Street and converted it into the Bowie Memorial Hospital. Dr. Fyke ran this hospital until 1945. That same year, the county purchased the building, renaming it Parker County Hospital. Remodeling and major additions followed and in 1958, the hospital changed names again. Dr. William Campbell, for whom the hospital is named, practiced medicine in Parker County for sixty-eight years and by his calculations, delivered more than five thousand babies during his extensive career as a doctor.

In 1968, the hospital board of directors selected a thirty-five acre tract of land bordering Eureka Street and Santa Fe Drive as a site for a new ninety-seven bed hospital. On November 9, 1972, Campbell Memorial Hospital opened its modern, well-equipped facility with a campus large enough to expand to meet the changing demands of healthcare. Growth continued as an ambulatory department formed in 1988, and the emergency department expanded in 1995.

In 2006, the hospital board leased the facility to what is now Medical City Weatherford. The Campbell Health System, now the Parker County Hospital District, continues in all of its public health phases and duties. This building continues to be a valuable resource for providing healthcare to the residents of Parker County and serves as a testament to the advancements in medical care in the area.

CHAPTER **21**
CITIZENS NATIONAL BANK

101 NORTH MAIN STREET

Citizens National Bank was built in 1868 by James Robertson Couts. It was the first bank built on the square. Couts was a Mason for thirty years and a member of the Methodist Episcopal Church. Born on April 6, 1833, in Robinson County, Tennessee, he was one of the wealthiest men in Parker County.

Until after the Civil War, banks in Texas were private merchant-related businesses that loaned money and kept the town's citizens' valuables in safes. While this bank can protect your money and valuables, it can't keep the loyal ghosts away.

The bank was especially important to the town. It was the talk of the town, but there were also whispers of a ghostly bank teller who haunted its halls that had been circulating since the 1880s. The bank tellers, managers, and security guards were extremely vigilant about the security of the building, and rightfully so. One day, as they arrived to open for business, they saw a man standing behind the teller window and immediately assumed they were being robbed. Frantically, they rushed in to apprehend the robber, but everything was to their surprise. The safe was secure, and there were no signs of forced entry. This strange occurrence repeated several times, leaving the employees completely baffled. After much contemplation, they concluded it could be the ghost of a loyal employee who had passed away. He continued to work at the bank out of pride and dedication even after death.

Citizens National Bank interior, 1884. *Courtesy of Special Collections UTA.*

A Texas State Historical Marker on site reads:

James Robertson Couts (1833–1904), a native of Tennessee, brought his family to Texas in 1858. Soon after the end of the Civil War, in which he served with a Texas frontier guard unit, Couts embarked on a long cattle drive to California. After wintering in Colorado and selling his stock in California, he returned to Weatherford in 1868 with $50,000 in gold. In partnership with John A. Fain, he set up the Couts and Fain Bank on the Courthouse Square.

By 1871 Fain had left the partnership and was succeeded by W.E. Hughes. At that time the bank was known as Hughes, Couts and Company. Two years later, Hughes left, and Couts' new partner was Henry Warren. The institution was renamed J.R. Couts and Company. By 1882 Warren had left the company. Couts applied for a federal banking charter, which was granted under the name Citizens National Bank.

A two-story stone building was completed on the corner of the Courthouse Square and N. Main Street in 1885. The bank continued to grow and prosper over the years, and in 1927 a merger was completed with the Parker County National Bank. Located in the same building for over one hundred years, Citizens National Bank is an important part of Weatherford's history.

CHAPTER 22

WEATHERFORD VINTAGE CAR MUSEUM, EVENT CENTER, AND GRILL

100 FORT WORTH HIGHWAY
MUSEUM: 817-550-6550
EVENT CENTER: 817-550-6612
WWW.VINTAGEWEATHERFORD.COM

Tom Moncrief and his wife, Therese, own the Vintage Car Museum, Event Center, and Grill. A lifelong admirer and collector of cars, Tom finally realized his dream and opened their nearly ten-thousand-square-foot museum in 2019. They brought back to life the abandoned buildings they purchased, creating an incredible experience for everyone and saving a bit more of historic Weatherford at the same time. You can see the beautiful courthouse just beyond when you drive up.

I have lost count of the number of times my family, friends, and I have eaten at the Grill next to the car museum. The restaurant has an award-winning chef, and the food is excellent. This alone would entice you to visit, but you can also check out the cars steps away while your food is prepared. You can't go wrong ordering anything off the menu. We often buy multiple dishes and taste a little of each.

The museum houses Moncrief's cars, of course, but visitors also enjoy seeing other people's collections featured there. Every time I visit, there's something new to see. Many of Tom and Therese's cars have an interesting story attached. He has the 1964 Lincoln Continental convertible that President Lyndon B. Johnson owned. It was used as Johnson's ranch car,

This page: Vintage Car Museum and Event Center.

and one thing is said: he loved to take guests around his ranch at high speeds. Years ago, as teenagers, we floated on innertubes down the river behind LBJ's place from a friend's house two doors down. It was very beautiful from the water. While the ranch was enormous, taking joyrides around must have been even more fun.

Another notable car is the Packard from *The Godfather*. You can see it in the movie in the scene where they say, "Leave the gun. Take the cannoli." People who enjoy *Pearl Harbor* will be excited to see a taxi from the film's making.

I enjoy visiting the museum, but I can't help but wonder if any ghosts also visit the vintage cars there. I have visited the museum with my friends several times, and we have all sensed a presence around us, even when we were alone. When we sit around the restaurant tables and share our experiences, we often realize that we all feel the same way. One time, two of my friends even saw someone sitting in one of the old cars, and they were worried that the person had entered the car without permission. However, the person disappeared into thin air when they approached the window. If you catch a glimpse of a ghost, notice the pure joy on their face as they revel in spending time with an old friend, their beloved car or truck. While you may not experience anything supernatural, it is worth a visit. The food is scrumptious, and the cars on display are truly remarkable. You won't be disappointed, that's for sure.

CHAPTER 23
KNIGHTS OF PYTHIAS LODGE

112 HOUSTON AVENUE

Knights of Pythias is a fraternal order established during the Civil War. The Pythians put their "Friendship, Charity, and Benevolence" motto into practice in Weatherford, helping many in need to this day. One place they held meetings was in the downtown building boasting a statue of a knight standing guard from the second floor facing the many who drive past the beautiful old building. Bennett's Office Supply has been operating out of the first floor of the downtown building for over sixty-two years. While nothing odd was reported to me about the downstairs, the upstairs, where the meetings used to take place, has had unexplained activity through the years.

People who went upstairs to look at the historic meeting spot were first surprised at how ample the space is, and then two of the property's viewers reported an unexplained chill that passed by. They oddly felt very comfortable and not at all frightened. They also reported hearing chairs being moved around, but the second floor was empty.

I was not surprised the unseen ghosts made them feel welcome. After all, they have a reputation for doing good and helping others.

They also built a beautiful castle on the hill on three hundred acres as a home for widows and orphans of Knights of Pythias members, which opened in 1909. The Texas Historical Marker at the Texas Pythian Home reads:

The Texas Grand Lodge of the Knights of Pythias considered building a home for dependent widows and children as early as 1886. In 1897, the Grand Lodge Convention started a fund-raising effort to establish such a home. Both the Knights and the Pythian Sisters of Texas contributed to the fund, and in 1905, the decision was made to find a location and to make plans for the construction of the home. The cornerstone for the massive main building was laid at this site near Weatherford in 1907. Of brick and stone construction, the building exhibits Moorish influences and contains 52 rooms. The first floor originally housed the girls' dormitory, a dining room, and the kitchen, while the second floor served as the boys' dormitory and contained an auditorium. Additional dormitory facilities were built later and are joined to the main building by arched walkways. Originally known as the "Widows and Orphans Home and Industrial School," the establishment opened in 1909, with the first residents coming from Amarillo, Sherman, and Beaumont. Over the years, it has served a great need in caring for dependent widows and orphans. The main building of the Texas Pythian Home has long been a landmark in Parker County. Texas Sesquicentennial 1836–1986.

Lone Star No. 4 Knights of Columbus Building.

CHAPTER 24
FRANCO-TEXAN LAND COMPANY BUILDING

118 HOUSTON AVENUE

The Franco-Texan Land Company Building has seen many generations pass through its historic doors. Tales are told of items moving independently and machines turning on by unseen hands. Old buildings sometimes have workers who always want to stay at their desks. Maybe this is a place just like that. It is a favorite building of mine.

I like where it sits in the historic downtown area, and I love the beautiful mural painted on one side of the building. It depicts the building as it would have proudly begun its long life in the emerging town filled with the brave pioneers who settled it.

There is a state historical marker on the site that reads:

In the late 19th century, this building was a center of political and economic life for Weatherford and Parker County. It was built around 1870. James Robertson Couts and John A. Fain established the first bank west of Dallas in this building, after Couts made a fortune selling cattle out west. Couts operated the bank with several partners, including Henry Warren, until 1877. Warren, a freighting contractor, and thoroughbred stockbreeder, had previously been associated with the Warren Freight Train Massacre of 1871.

Couts and Warren dissolved their professional relationship in 1877 and sold the building to Samuel Willis Tucker Lanham, later governor of

Above: Franco-Texan Land Company Building.

Right: Historic marker for Franco-Texan Land Company Building.

FRANCO-TEXAN LAND
COMPANY BUILDING

IN THE LATE 19TH CENTURY, THIS BUILDING WAS A CENTER FOR
POLITICAL AND ECONOMIC LIFE FOR THE TOWN OF WEATHERFORD
AND FOR PARKER COUNTY. IT WAS BUILT AROUND 1870. JAMES
ROBERTSON COUTS AND JOHN A. FAIN ESTABLISHED THE FIRST BANK
WEST OF DALLAS IN THIS BUILDING. AFTER COUTS MADE A "FORTUNE
SELLING CATTLE OUT WEST. COUTS OPERATED THE BANK WITH
SEVERAL PARTNERS, INCLUDING HENRY WARREN, UNTIL 1877.
WARREN, A FREIGHTING CONTRACTOR AND THOROUGHBRED
STOCKBREEDER, HAD PREVIOUSLY BEEN ASSOCIATED WITH THE
WARREN FREIGHT TRAIN MASSACRE OF 1871.

COUTS AND WARREN DISSOLVED THEIR PROFESSIONAL
RELATIONSHIP IN 1877 AND SOLD THE BUILDING TO SAMUEL WILLIS
TUCKER LANHAM, LATER GOVERNOR OF TEXAS (1903-1907). LANHAM
PRACTICED LAW WITH OTHER ATTORNEYS, SUCH AS A.J. HOOD SR.,
IN SECOND STORY OFFICES. DURING THE 1890s, THE STRUCTURE
SERVED AS THE OFFICES FOR THE TROUBLED FRANCO-TEXAN LAND
COMPANY, HEADED BY HOOD. THE COMPANY WAS INTEGRAL IN THE
DEVELOPMENT OF TEXAS LAND BETWEEN WEATHERFORD AND EL
PASO ALONG THE TEXAS AND PACIFIC RAILWAY CORRIDOR. DURING
THIS PERIOD THE SAFE, FROM THE FIDELITY AND SAFE DEPOSIT
COMPANY, WAS INSTALLED AT THE REAR OF THE BUILDING. S.W.T.
LANHAM SOLD THE PROPERTY IN 1906 TO WILLIAM BOONE.

THE FRANCO-TEXAN LAND COMPANY BUILDING, PREVIOUSLY
KNOWN AS THE COUTS BUILDING AND THE WESTERN UNION
BUILDING, IS AN EXAMPLE OF A TYPICAL VERNACULAR STOREFRONT
COMMERCIAL BUILDING FOUND IN TEXAS DURING THE LAST
QUARTER OF THE 19TH CENTURY. THE TWO-STORY MASONRY
FRONTED BUILDING FEATURES A BRICK EXTERIOR, STONE STRING
COURSES, FRENCH DOORS WITH FANLIGHT TRANSOMS, AND
DOUBLE-HUNG WINDOWS.

RECORDED TEXAS HISTORIC LANDMARK 2012
MARKER IS PROPERTY OF THE STATE OF TEXAS

Texas (1903–1907). Lanham practiced law with other attorneys, such as A.J. Hood Sr., in second-story offices. During the 1890s, the structure served as the offices for the troubled Franco-Texan Land Company, headed by Hood. The company was integral in the development of Texas land between Weatherford and El Paso along the Texas and Pacific Railway corridor. During this period the safe, from the Fidelity and Safe Deposit Company, was installed at the rear of the building.

S.W.T. Lanham sold the property in 1906 to William Boone.

The Franco-Texan Land Company Building, previously known as the Couts Building and the Western Union Building, is an example of a typical vernacular storefront commercial building found in Texas during the last quarter of the 19th century. The two-story masonry-fronted building features a brick exterior, stone string courses, French doors with fanlight transoms, and double-hung windows.

CHAPTER 25
202 WEST OAK STREET

This pretty Victorian house might be home to a ghost as well as being the administrative building for the Weatherford Fire Department. The home, built in 1899, has left a legacy of stories from various owners, neighbors, and people who had experiences while visiting the house. It once belonged to the family of U.S. Speaker of the House Jim Wright. It was purchased in 2009 by the City of Weatherford. As with any home of this age, there have been deaths, accidents, and significant life experiences that I believe have imprinted themselves onto the property, house, or land, with or without the building still standing.

The same stories pass through generations of believers in this house's resident ghosts. I spoke with a woman who lived there for a short while, and she remembers on several occasions watching from the upstairs stairway into the living room and seeing a figure of a woman who seemed to be sweeping. This ghost never noticed the little girl watching while she worked. Her mother never saw the lady of the house but did encounter the ghosts of three little children watching her from the top of the stairs. At first, she thought it was her children, but she reminded them to be careful up there. She heard giggles from the top of the stairs just as her children entered through the back door. She was so unnerved by the incident that they moved soon after.

There are unexplained and sudden cold spots, as well as sounds of creaking boards accompanied by footsteps with no physical body attached. Lights are left on, and when a person returns to the room, they have been turned off, and vice versa. Doors are heard opening and closing when no other person is home to make that happen. Disembodied voices have been heard calling a living person's name. While all the experiences are startling, nothing negative has ever been reported. Sometimes, spirits want to be acknowledged. Other times, it is all coincidental; visitors are moving through a memory of when they existed. It could also be an intelligent haunting, an imprint left in that space by another person or animal that lived there.

CHAPTER 26
FIRST MONDAY "STRAY DAYS"

317 SANTA FE DRIVE

Weatherford enjoys a pioneer tradition from the 1850s originally called the First Monday Stray Day Sale. This encompassing event saw farmers and townsfolk gather at the town square to trade or sell their handmade goods, fresh garden produce, and milk from their goats and cows. It was also a time for legal matters to be handled at the courthouse. The event attracted large crowds from all over Texas and neighboring territories, and it still holds the title of one of the oldest open-air markets in Texas.

The tradition lives on today, with a change to its name to First Monday Trade Days, but it maintains the roots of the original pioneer gathering. It is held the weekend before the first Monday of each month. The event is a delightful mix of old and new, with vendors offering antiques, arts and crafts, and delicious food. It's a fun-filled event with a lot to explore and enjoy—but beware of ghost vendors and buy from live traders.

Stories of people chatting with or purchasing from a ghost have circulated since the late 1800s. It's said the sheriff once had to resolve a disagreement over payment for goods. Upon cooler heads prevailing, the buyer saw where the ghost, as it turned out, put the cash. The merchant set his proclamation that he would never hide his cash in the cornmeal bag and was astonished to have the sheriff find the coins inside for the very amount the buyer claimed to have paid. The matter was settled with handshakes and head scratches as the "darndest thing."

Chicken seller, historic 1930s First Monday Trade Days.

Grains, beans, and eggs seller, historic 1930s First Monday Trade Days.

Horse traders and sellers at the historic 1939 First Monday Trade Days.

Visitors today claim to see people dressed like pioneers folding quilts and stocking shelves, but when they get to the stall, no one dressed like that is anywhere to be found. It's sometimes hard to tell the living from the dead when the manner of dress hasn't changed that much at certain events filled with modern-day cowboys and cowgirls mixed with reenactors and, of course, ghosts.

CHAPTER 27

THE DOUBLE CABIN
AT HOLLAND LAKE

1400 TEXAS DRIVE

The historic double cabin at Holland Lake has since been moved, but when it was located at 1400 Texas Drive by the much-visited lake, ghostly figures were seen sitting in the cabin's breezeway for decades. Is this George McCleskey happily enjoying his life before it was cut short? There have also been reports of people dressed in old-fashioned clothing working and gardening around the cabin. When approached by people, they vanish. I'm curious if the sightings continue now that the cabin has been moved to its new location, sharing space with other historic cabins in Weatherford.

A marker was placed at the original cabin that reads: "A monument to the pioneers of Parker County. The east room with bullet scarred walls shows where George McCleskey was killed by Indians in 1873. The west room was Dan Waggoner's headquarters ranch house, built in 1855. Adopted meeting place for Old Settlers Reunions."

One and a half miles away from 1400 Texas Drive is the Woolfolk-McCall House. It belonged to one of the two attorneys in the town who defended two Native Americans accused of mass murders of settlers traveling on a wagon train to the area. The marker at 202 South Waco in Weatherford reads:

One of the first brick homes in Weatherford, this structure was begun in late 1860s and occupied by Joseph A. Woolfolk (1836–1918), one of two attorneys who defended Indian Chiefs Satanta and Big Tree, charged in 1871 wagon train massacre. In 1879 it was purchased by lawyer George A. McCall (1849–1915) and greatly enlarged with stone and frame additions. After almost 100 years of ownership, the McCall family sold the house in 1972 to Mr. and Mrs. Douglas Wiley.

The trial of Satanta and Big Tree occurred in 1871 in the town of Jacksboro in Jackson County, Texas. This historic trial of Native American war chiefs of the Kiowa Indians was for the murder of seven teamsters during a raid on Salt Creek Prairie. Henry Warren was contracted to haul supplies to the forts in West Texas, including Fort Richardson, Fort Griffin, and Fort Concho, traveling down the Jacksboro Belknap Road heading toward Salt Creek. Fort Richardson, active between 1867 and 1878, is just forty-four miles from Holland Lake. Fort Concho, active between 1867 and 1889, is where I have family ties; it is worth a visit and is just an additional 213 miles away.

Captain Henry Warren erected a painted wooden monument where the raid occurred. The sign has disappeared, but his journal entry reads as follows:

I Came to the Monument area and discovered seven men massacred fifty yards on the left side of the road. 18 May 1871—Inscribed as follows: Sacred to the memory of seven brave men killed by Indians at this place on Thurs. May 18, 1871, while in the discharge of their duty, defending their train against one hundred and fifty Comanche Indians. N.S. Song— Wagon Master. Teamsters: J.S. Elliott, Sam Elliott, N.J. Baxter, Jas Williams, John Mullins, Jesse Bowman.

This was the first time the United States had tried Native American chiefs in a state court. The trial attracted national and international attention. The Native Americans accused were formally indicted on July 1, 1871, and tried shortly thereafter for acts arising out of the Warren wagon train raid. They were given a sentence worse than death in their minds: life in prison.

Now, back to that haunted lake. Other lakes around the country have their ghost stories about a lady of the lake. Holland Lake is no exception. Rumors persist about a woman seen roaming the lake dripping wet and seemingly confused and lost. Whenever help is offered, she looks at the person, startled, and then vanishes before their eyes. Is this perhaps the ghost of a drowning victim, or was something more sinister at play that took their life? We will never know.

Holland's Lake, Weatherford, Texas

Holland Lake postcard.

Another story circulates about the Holland Lake area that locals have whispered for generations. A bridge off Dennis Road spans part of the Brazos River. People claim to see a goat man around the Brazos River and tree-lined spots surrounding it. People often fish in this area, and many hear heavy steps going through brush and rocks heading toward them.

There have been times when people saw something that appeared to be a half goat, half man standing upright as if it were human. It makes loud goat screams as it chases them from their favorite fishing spot. It's not just fishermen who have encountered this entity. People who hike around the historic area have also heard the loud screaming sound of a goat and sometimes even glimpsed a hairy upright figure that may just have been an encounter with the Goatman.

Another spot people say is haunted is an overpass drainage tunnel next to Holland Lake. The kids call it a graffiti tunnel. Youths have seen things moving down the tunnel when no other people are around. They've seen shadow people and heard disembodied voices yelling to them, "Get out!" Some say a young male has been seen in that area several times but vanishes before their eyes when spoken to.

CHAPTER 28

HAUNTED AMUSEMENT PARK

1701 EAST LANCASTER AVENUE, FORT WORTH

Cutting Edge Haunted House was voted best in the nation in 2023. It is a haunted attraction based in the first slaughterhouse in Fort Worth. Live actors, special effects, and created monsters all help to create this intense multi-themed attraction full of chills, screams, and big scares.

Knowing people who have worked there that I trust, I believe all the haunted stories from that place. This haunted house is located in an over one-hundred-year-old abandoned meatpacking plant in a section of Fort Worth that was historically called "Hell's Half Acre." It's built on a foundation of blood and fear from the uncountable animals slaughtered there. All the meatpacking equipment from the Old West days is still there and used as part of a scare while going through the building. Nowadays, instead of processing cattle fearfully crying out as they are shuttled through the cattle yards into their final moments of life, humans are running through its corridors screaming at the actors as they jump out at them or the many terrifying sights they pass by until the doors open to let them out—a grace the cattle never received.

The haunted house uses old equipment with realistic-looking mannequins hoisted up to the second level and brought through the entire process that the meatpacking plant used to use. For the ultimate scare at the end, the conveyor system brings the butchered corpses back to the first level. It takes about an hour to go through Cutting Edge Haunted House. I could make it in half that time, as scary as it sounds.

In all seriousness, this attraction has gained a reputation for being one of the country's best scary places to visit and one of the biggest and most haunted houses. I was happy to hear they care about the people who work for them and those who visit there. I think that when you care, it makes such a difference. The operators want to ensure that everyone has a lot of fun and that things are very safe.

As a notorious part of Fort Worth's history, the location has captivated everyone's minds since the late 1870s. Hell's Half Acre was a rest stop along the cattle trails from Texas to Kansas, a place that transformed from dusty cattle pens into a half acre bustling with brothels, saloons, and liquor flowing as men gambled and wanted to one-up the next guy. It was initially set out to go from 10th Street to 15th Street, intersecting Houston Street, Rusk Street, and Main Street. The Chisholm Trail and Texas and Pacific Railways helped boost its growth. They brought in many Old West gunslingers and cowboys, some even famous, including Butch Cassidy, Wyatt Earp, Doc Holliday, and Bat Masterson.

It earned the title of the town's bloody third ward due to so much lawlessness and violence in such a small square footage. Speaking of small square footage, it is twenty-two thousand square feet, but packed within were violent criminals and thieves mixed with good people who were just cowboys driving the cattle along the trail to get paid. Businessmen had to be there to move the cattle and buy them, so it was a real mix of people. The gambling parlors, hotels, saloons, and bordellos were all part of it. There is one saloon that stands out and has always been known in the area, and it is called the White Elephant Saloon. It was beautiful and filled with gunfights, dancing in the streets, and music from the different establishments, all mingling to heighten the intensity of the mood of the wild souls.

However, in the twentieth century, the acre's popularity fell off, things began to be more progressive, and the lawlessness was being contained to a greater level. After 1889, officials cracked down, and by 1919, Fort Worth had said no more. The third ward was changed and brought into a much more orderly, law-abiding part of Fort Worth. While its testament to the Wild West era is true and remains, it's also a beautiful area with much commerce and family activities.

There is a Texas State Historical Marker in the bloody Hell's Half Acre that reads:

A notorious red light district known as Hell's Half Acre developed in this section of Fort Worth after the arrival of the Texas and Pacific Railway in 1876 launched a local economic boom. Fort Worth was soon the favorite destination for hundreds of cowboys, buffalo hunters, railroad workers, and freighters eager to wash off the trail dust and enjoy themselves. To meet the demand, a large number of saloons, dance halls, gambling houses, and bordellos opened between the Courthouse Square and the railroad depot. Illegal activities in Hell's Half Acre were tolerated by city officials because of their importance to the town's economy. The district prospered in the 1880s and added to Fort Worth's growing reputation as a rowdy frontier town. Famous gamblers Luke Short, Bat Masterson and Wyatt Earp and outlaws Sam Bass, Eugene Bunch, Butch Cassidy and the Sundance Kid are known to have spent time in Hell's Half Acre. A 1906 newspaper headline calling the district Fort Worth's den of sin and refuge of criminals was representative of periodic efforts to clean up the district. These efforts proved unsuccessful until Army officials at Camp Bowie, established here during World War I, helped local officials shut the district down.

Aside from being the spot of Cutting Edge Haunted House and its hauntings, Hell's Half Acre is filled with its own ghost stories. For decades, the ghosts of gunslingers have been seen appearing and disappearing through walls, and many voices have been heard calling out, "Hey!" as people pass by, but nobody who's living is attached to the voice. Ghostly sounds from the past include horse's hooves, the jingle of spurs, and the hum of a crowd of people murmuring private conversations and laughing, as well as screams ringing out from female and male voices. As it would have been in those gambling saloons, all mix into the night air, at times echoing the past ghostly voices carried in the wind to this day.

Many people have reported being pushed on the stairs in various businesses, seeing things move, glasses shattering for no reason, and seeing shadows and sometimes full-body apparitions. But you have to think about how there was so much activity in such a small space. All the emotions that go into that imprint into those buildings and the dirt that the blood ran into from those unfortunate gunfights, fistfights, and murders among men and of the prostitutes brought in for the cowboys' entertainment after the long cattle drives. You can't have that many lawless acts without repercussions. That small space of the historic town of Fort Worth has seen its fair share of deaths, murders, and attacks inside the buildings and on the streets and dark alleyways.

There is a room at Cutting Edge called the drum stage. During the weekend, drummers play, and people are also put into groups as they go through the slaughterhouse. One night, before the amusement park opened across the room, my friend thought she was the only one in this backstage space. She noticed a very solid figure all in black clothing. She couldn't see his face because of how his head was turned, but she didn't think anything of it. She thought it was a new security guard she did not know; maybe somebody was starting work that night. The figure turned and stared at her with fog and flashing lights mixed in. It felt odd, but he just kept staring at her. She called out several times, saying, "Hello, are you new to working here? Do you need help finding the area you are supposed to work in?" But there was never an answer as she approached the figure, thinking he might not hear her since all the noise and music had kicked up, getting ready to open. The closer she got, the man's stares never stopped; however, before she could get any closer, she noticed the lower half of the person's body was not there, and then he turned and walked right through the wall in front of her eyes.

That room leads into a space where they used to butcher the cattle. The original butcher block is there, and the hanging hooks are still in working order. Several times when my friend worked there, that man in black by the butcher block could be seen, always just taking in the crowd, appearing to be watching all the happenings. At times, he was joined by other people who were shadowing behind him. It seemed to be a group of ghostly overseers. There was one entity on the third floor that many people have seen. It looks like a moving, flowing black fog, never fully formed yet taking on a sort of image as it moves of a body climbing across the walls of the building. Everybody who has seen this entity had the distinct feeling that it was evil. Unlike the ghost in black who seems to watch what's happening, this third-floor entity is not one you want to encounter. Customers who have reported seeing this creepy dark spirit crawling across the walls thought it was just part of the well-crafted scares this place offers. Little did they know they had encountered a real dark spirit.

Have a wonderful visit to this amusement park. Keep a close eye out, though, because you might think another person is going through the haunted house with you, but it may just be a ghost or something more sinister.

CHAPTER **29**

VEAL'S STATION AND CEMETERY

2900 VEAL STATION ROAD, SPRINGTOWN

Veal's Station is just twelve miles north of Weatherford and is one of the oldest settlements in Parker County. For many years, it has been surrounded by mystery and ghostly legends. Stories of unexplained lights, shadowy figures, and eerie whistling have been passed down for generations, even as far back as the late 1800s. Ghostly figures watch from their tombstones as people walk through the cemetery.

This area was a beautiful place to build a community. It looked down a valley near the Trinity River on one side and part of Walnut Creek on the other. Lining the beautiful waterways were endless walnut trees from which to eat and bake. The area was a rich resource of water and food, as well as many trees for building homes and businesses for the pioneers making a life in this area.

One of the first white settlers arriving in the area in the 1850s was Captain William G. Veal. He was a Mason and helped the Masonic Lodge, known as Eureka Lodge, operate there between 1860 and 1873. It was said he played a part in helping to organize several lodges in Texas. He was also a Methodist minister and, throughout his lifetime, preached at many churches in many different towns. Still, he always returned to his beloved Veal's Station whenever he could to minister. He opened a general store less than a mile away, referred to at the time as Cream Hill. In 1857, he moved it to the large building he and fellow settlers G.W. Coleman and John Lantz built, which was in those times a meetinghouse to cover many needs under one roof. It was a school, church, town hall, and Masonic meeting hall. They brought all the buildings close together to protect those settling the land from Native American attacks.

William and Elisabeth Woody were essential to the settlement of Veal's Station and were buried in Veal Station Cemetery. Once their house was complete, it served several distinct and important purposes for the Veal's Station community. The property was used as a refuge, a stagecoach stop for pioneer travelers, a boardinghouse for college students attending Parsons College, a community meeting place for all religious denominations in the area, and a cobbler's workshop for boots and shoes.

In 1857, the community added a short-lived postal service. This was unsustainable due to the continued attacks on the settlers. By the late 1870s, the settlers had successfully claimed the area safe from further threats, and postal service resumed in 1878. Having a connection to the world left behind by the settlers helped the area grow and thrive as a busy farming community. Two cotton gins were built and processed the crops from area farmers.

Sadly, the town was not picked as a stop for the railroad, and it began once again to slip away from progress to its quiet beginnings.

One of the most intriguing tales haunting this historic town is the legend of the ghost lights of Veal's Station. According to local folklore, many residents and visitors have witnessed these mysterious lights, often described as orbs of flickering light that float and dance in the distance. These ethereal lights have both fascinated and terrified those who have encountered them. What could they be? Are they orbs or phantom lanterns carried by the settlers just going about their business as if they were still alive?

Ghost hunters come to Veal's Station, hoping to glimpse these otherworldly lights. The feelings associated with those who claim to have witnessed them vary from a sense of awe and wonder to an eerie presence. Many have tried to capture the phenomenon on camera, but the lights always seem to elude them, adding to their mystique. Whether you believe in the supernatural or not, the ghost lights of Veal's Station remain an enduring part of Weatherford's ghostly folklore. Veal's Station invites you to unravel the mystery of its ghost lights and experience the thrill of the unknown.

Another haunted spot is the Veal Station Cemetery, a burial ground said to be haunted by the ghost of a young girl who tragically lost her life in a fire. Visitors have reported hearing her laughter and seeing her apparition skipping among the tombstones, creating an ethereal atmosphere that sends shivers down the spine.

The whistler spirit is a legend attached to several places in the cemetery. The distinct whistling of a partial tune, not just a note or two, has been reportedly heard when no one else is there. It has been heard at the far back of the cemetery and seems to move too quickly to be explained easily as just a hiding person playing a prank. Some have tried to explain it away as a bird song or a train whistle, but those don't carry the same tone as a human voice whistle, and remember, it's heard as a partial song that nobody can place up to this point. Maybe one day, it will be captured on a recording and identified as a known song or familiar tune from a time long ago.

One tale often told, even on the local news, is that of a tombstone seen to glow. Well, this could be one light people are seeing. It belongs to William E. Wright, who was born on September 29, 1912, and passed on July 18, 1931, at age nineteen. The glowing tombstone is nestled in the southeast corner of the cemetery. I couldn't see it during my visits, but many claim to have witnessed it. I hope you see it for yourself.

I have visited the cemetery twice and never caught anything that is usually reported, and unfortunately, I never saw the mysterious lights. But a friend was present, and we heard the sound of someone running toward us when no other visitors were in the cemetery, so I'll keep trying. If you venture out, remember the cemetery gates are locked at sunset. You can, however, park outside the locked gates and peer into the cemetery from the safety of your car. I have done this myself.

There is a Texas Historical Marker at Veal Station Cemetery that reads:

> The community of Veal's Station developed by 1851 in northeastern Parker County and became a stop on the stagecoach line running from Fort Worth to Fort Richardson. The settlement took the name of William G. Veal and thrived as an educational and religious center, with Veal's Station College, Parsons College, and a masonic institute in operation from the 1850s to the early 1900s. The population declined after many of the school buildings burned.
>
> When early settler William Woody patented 320 acres in the area in 1857, a corner of his field already contained primitive graves marked by native stones. Woody established a community cemetery at that site in 1857, with the first known burial, for Mary Ann Broils Rector, occurring the following year. Other notable burials include early settler Martha Cockburn Tucker; cemetery founder William Woody and his wife, Elisabeth; Joseph Looney Woody, a participant in the 1869 Little Salt Creek Indian fight;

and county commissioner Jesse Andrew Gilley and his wife, Missouri Gilley, who was a Delaware Indian.

Veal's Station Cemetery comprises approximately 2.7 acres and more than 740 burials. Numerous pioneer families, early postmasters, veterans from the Civil War to Vietnam, elected officials, clergy, teachers, and members of fraternal organizations are among those interred here. It remains an active burial ground today, cared for by the Veal's Station community, which began annual cemetery meetings by 1942.

The Texas Historical Marker at the William and Elisabeth Woody Homestead reads:

William (Bill) Woody (1824–1915), one of the first Anglo settlers in Parker County, was born in Roane County, Tennessee. While living in the eastern Tennessee hills bordering North Carolina, he married Elisabeth Lydia Farmer (1822–1879) in 1846. In December 1846, six weeks after the birth of their son, the Woody family set out to Texas on foot with few possessions. Six months later, they arrived in Honey Grove in Fannin County, where they met up with other family members and established a working farm. In 1851, the family traveled to White Settlement in Tarrant County where they stayed until their home was built here by 1855. Located in the Veal's Station Community, the Woody family built a story-and-a-half, four-room dogtrot home using hand-sawn yellow pine lumber transported by ox from New Orleans.

Once their house was complete, it served several distinct and important purposes for the Veal's Station Community. The property was used as a refuge and stagecoach stop for pioneer travelers, a boarding house for college students attending Parsons College, and a community meeting place for all religious denominations in the area, as well as a cobbler's workshop for hand-cobbled boots and shoes. In 1858, Bill Woody and community members built a two-story frame meeting house on the property which provided a church, masonic hall, town hall, common school, and later Parsons College, chartered in 1874, for the town of Veal's Station. Elisabeth and Bill Woody are buried in the Veal's Station Cemetery, both examples of rugged individualism that expanded the state and country in the nineteenth century.

CHAPTER 30
HAUNTED HILL HOUSE

501 NORTHEAST FIRST STREET, MINERAL WELLS
817-884-7152
HAUNTEDHILLHOUSE.COM

This 133-year-old home is one of the most haunted locations in the country. I have visited many sites worldwide and have never experienced this level of haunting at another location, day or night. This historic house is filled with emotions from entities, suicides, murders, dark magic, and love. A beautiful pair of caring guardians, Kathy and Sonny Estes, show unmistakable love and protectiveness toward the spirits of their acquired property.

They told me how they learned about the beautiful and haunted mansion. "A paranormal team showed us pictures of three kids: a girl and two little boys. We looked at the picture and said, 'Well, that's cool, little kids.' And he goes, 'No, those aren't kids. You can see right through them. Look at them.' And we're like, 'Oh my God, they looked like they were real kids!' We asked where it was from. And he said, 'That's from this place called the Haunted Hill House, and this was taken in the Carousel Room.'" When Kathy and Sonny first visited the home, they saw with their own eyes a green orb turn into a greenish-colored little boy. He walked up the stairs and stood next to them. "Then we heard voices. It was an amazing visit."

Hill House is opposite historic East Mountain, one of the original sites of the "Welcome Sign" and three wells. It's worth mentioning the wells on the property, as they are often considered a factor in hauntings because their power is used as a conduit for energy; they are believed to be portals to other dimensions. Spirits are said to communicate through water and electricity, which is why many ghost encounters occur on dark and stormy nights.

The East Mountain caves at the back of the property have their own haunted past. According to local lore, Native Americans stayed in these caves and fought against settlers they saw as invaders of their lands. I learned this information when I visited Hill House and saw a vision of a line of Native Americans on horseback in front of East Mountain. The vision was so clear that I stopped mid-sentence when speaking with Kathy and Sonny. The line of Native Americans was in the trees, in front of the mountains, all lined up watching me, maybe waiting to see my reaction. Being part Native American myself, it was thrilling to see them, and I felt honored to have experienced this.

The rider in front wore a full headdress and buckskin pants adorned with beads and fringe. His moccasins were a reddish-tan color but were covered in a chalk-like dust. Two other men dressed more plainly were on horseback to his left side, and one similarly dressed with fewer feathers in his headdress was on horseback to his right. There were younger males on foot just a few feet behind the group. It was such a powerful visitation by these spirits that I would have believed them to be reenactors rather than ghosts.

Other visitors besides myself have seen them at Hill House. Their most active time to show themselves is dusk or early morning. I saw them at sunset, and they stared at me, only moving slightly for several minutes. They seemed more curious than anything else that I could see them.

Kathy Estes has seen them in the exact location and in the same lineup I did. Is this a residual haunting encounter or an intelligent one? Further investigation is needed to determine that.

On one occasion, when visiting Hill House, I was relentlessly bombarded with visions of a train running right by the house. I had never heard of a train robbery near the house or anything like that. Even so, I have learned through the years to trust what the spirits tell me, especially those residing at Hill House. They are such tattletales!

I kept seeing a train being robbed. I told Kathy and Sonny about this, and they told me you can see the remnants of the train tracks near the home. They have found train spikes and other items on the property. They even have an EVP of a child yelling out, "Look, they're robbing the train!"

A jewel thief trying to hide his bounty from several heists supposedly lost his life in one of the caves behind the house after being stuck between several boulders that fell on him as he was climbing down from a high ledge. Maybe this is the spirit I sensed lurking just inside the mouth of a cave.

The town of Mineral Wells owes its identity and prosperity to the mineral waters that brought in many visitors during the first sixty years of its existence. Interestingly, many hauntings and paranormal occurrences have been reported around Mineral Wells. This is because flowing water is essentially energy, and underground water, coupled with the high volume of limestone deposits in Texas, creates the perfect environment for paranormal activity. Similar occurrences are observed in other towns and areas around the United States and other countries built on top of natural water sources.

It is believed that stone, specifically limestone, can act as a "recorder" of energy, so residual hauntings are common in places where limestone is present. Residual hauntings are not intelligent and typically involve ghosts that do not interact with the living. They appear as if on a recorded loop playing out the actions they took in life. Mineral Wells has many buildings made of limestone, and coupled with the presence of limestone underground, this explains why there are many reports of residual ghosts in the town. These ghosts are seen in hallways, on stairs, crossing the street, walking through walls, and so on.

Some residual hauntings involve ghosts that repeatedly play out their final moments. For example, my friend folklorist Susan Hill has lived right down the road from Mineral Wells her whole life and tells me when you go through those mountains into the town, there is a noticeable change in energy. The town feels different. I have to agree with that. It seems like the town takes you back through a time portal. She has had many experiences at Hill House. She saw a woman in a dark Victorian dress several times in the backyard of Hill House. This ghost is usually off to the right if you look out the back door, and she always takes the same path without interacting with anyone.

Mineral water popularity started to decline during the 1930s. One legend about Hill House is that it was used as a bootlegging operation during Prohibition between 1920 and 1933. The occupants of Hill House back then were more interested in indulging in illegal alcohol and gambling than worrying about the stock market.

Several accidental deaths happened on the property, and information about them can be found in old newspaper articles and death records. A man working on the chimney fell off the roof to his death in the 1950s. A little girl named Madeline was playing ball across the street. She was hit by a car while chasing it to Hill House and died on the steps by the front door. She is often seen and picked up by various methods used in investigations. On my first visit, I saw her standing on the curb holding a ball. I did not know this story then, so I believe she appeared to me as to others encountering her.

The gambling room, or the Scratcher Room as it is now referred to, is still present in Hill House. Here, money flowed freely across the card tables as ladies of the night entertained themselves. Some believe their spirits never left. The Scratcher Room is always an active space. Many paranormal teams have similar experiences here. I was present when my friend, author and paranormal investigator Martha Hazzard Decker, was scratched. Long bleeding scratches formed when her hands were visible on the card table. Nothing near her could have caused the scratches. One characteristic I have noted is that the scratches worsen as minutes pass if the person does not leave the room.

That night, while using different devices to communicate with the spirits, I felt something like little nails running down my right leg and several spots on my back. It stung more than hurt, but I left the room, and several people witnessed the red marks on me.

Jeannie Van Hoose was investigating with her team, and this is what they experienced in the Scratcher Room. We sat down at a simple card table and began to attempt communication with any spirits that occupied the space. All our instruments were activated immediately, and the temperature dropped to a chill. Some of our group felt unseen forces among us were physically touching them. One of our members was painfully scratched down the arm, and an object forcefully flew from an open closet across the room. We then received an EVP of a low, angry growl that could have been any sinister entity within the house, including the demon who calls himself "Toby." We ended our investigation in the Scratcher Room after receiving that EVP. The investigation continued to be highly active throughout the evening.

Jeannie and her group encountered the ghost of a little boy named Joshua. Joshua even opened a door for us when we asked him to play. The movement of solid objects, such as doors, requires tremendous energy from spirits, so this was extremely impressive and demonstrated Joshua's strength of energy. We then asked him to touch a device called a REM pod that detects air temperature changes. If the temperature changes five degrees or more, an alarm is sounded. We also filmed the encounter with an SLS camera developed by the military to help soldiers visualize opponents in unclear conditions. When entities are detected on this variety of cameras, they appear as stick figures and show size, placement, and movement. In reviewing our SLS camera footage, we could see Joshua's spirit, in this form, touch the REM pod with his hand. In the video, when Joshua's hand reached the device, the REM pod sounded loudly at the exact moment. Seeing this little boy walk up to the REM pod and activate it was the most spectacular, rewarding experience I have ever had as a paranormal investigator.

There are too many experiences to add here, but book your investigation at Haunted Hill House with Kathy and Sonny Estes. You won't be disappointed.

AFTERWORD

I hope you have enjoyed the stories and have some new places to add to your list to visit. Please remember that some of the places mentioned in this book are private property, and some have hours of operation to make note of. Please always remember to ask permission to take pictures or investigate a property.

I wanted to include a protection prayer for those who believe in them. I use them along with common sense when investigating a cemetery or building. Remember to let people know where you are going. If possible, don't investigate alone. Even seasoned investigators travel in pairs or groups. Carry a flashlight, extra batteries, and a first aid kit to be prepared. You can capture evidence and record from most cellphones if you don't have paranormal investigation equipment.

After you do a paranormal investigation, it is important to cleanse yourself and your equipment. Here is a cautionary tale about forgetting to cleanse yourself and your belongings. Jamie Mose, a paranormal investigator friend, and I were so caught up discussing our many interactions with spirits at Haunted Hill House in Mineral Wells and the short time until her next investigation later that day that we did not practice what I preach.

It wasn't long before we knew we were not alone in her car. Besides the odd feeling of shared space with an invisible rider, the spirit wanted to be sure we knew it was along for the ride. My mobile phone started to growl. I knew immediately that the demon Toby had made himself known to me the night before. Jamie and I looked at each other, commenting only after the third growl. We checked for odd charger connections; no radio was playing, and we even got desperate for road noise or window vibration. All the time, we knew it was Toby. The growls were a signature sound, like a voice. These were something oddly mixed between human and animal, close and yet far away at the same time.

The timing of its responses to our conversation became unnerving, to the point that we stopped at a church before we reached our home destination and used my personal mix of holy water and oils to cleanse my phone, ourselves, the car, and all its contents. We could feel the energy move away immediately. Once we settled back inside, we felt different, as did the space within the car.

Prayer of Protection
One of the most powerful and called upon Archangels is Saint Michael. People often use this prayer before and after they go on paranormal investigations, but of course, it can be used for your request for protection at any time or situation.

Opening Prayer
Saint Michael the Archangel defends us in battle,
Be our protection against the wickedness and snares of the Devil,
May God rebuke him, we humbly pray,
And do thou, O Prince of the heavenly host,
By the power of God, thrust into hell Satan and all evil spirits
Who wanders through the world for the ruin of souls.
Amen

Closing prayer
In the name of Jesus Christ, I command all human spirits to be bound to the confines of the cemetery [or wherever you are investigating].
I command all inhuman spirits to go where Jesus Christ tells you to go, for He commands you.
Amen

BIBLIOGRAPHY

May, David. "Your Family: Heavenly Hauntings." *Weatherford Democrat*, October 22, 2013. www.weatherforddemocrat.com/news/local_news/your-family-heavenly-hauntings/article_34725725-871d-5e83-aceb-be0a98fd18e8.html

Newspapers. newspapers.com.

Parker County Heritage Society. www.parkercountyheritagesociety.com.

Texas Historical Commission. "Historical Markers." thc.texas.gov/preserve/preservation-programs/historical-markers.

Texas State Historical Association. "Hartnett, Jeffrey Aloysius (1859–1899)." www.tshaonline.org/handbook/entries/hartnett-jeffrey-aloysius.

Texas State Library and Archives Commission. www.tsl.texas.gov.

Vintage Car Museum. vintageweatherford.com/museum.

Weatherford. weatherfordtx.gov.

Wikipedia. "Weatherford, Texas." en.wikipedia.org/wiki/Weatherford, Texas.

ABOUT THE AUTHOR

Teal Gray is a best-selling native Texan author and sacred site traveler. She is an ordained minister fascinated with world religions and their varying belief systems. Teal has used her gift of intuition and mediumship to help many paranormal investigative teams everywhere, from historic buildings to homes around the world and sacred sites. Through these many experiences, she has amassed a greater understanding of the unknown. Sharing that knowledge is her passion. Ever curious, she hopes to make your reading experience feel like you are on the trail of answers with her.